YOUR HOUSE AT THE BEACH:
FINDING IT, BUYING IT, AND OPERATING IT

BY

Barbara D. Ingersoll and Betsy S. Davis

Published by Cape Publications, Incorporated

Reproduction or translation of any part of this work beyond that permitted by Section 107 or 108 of the 1976 United States Copyright Act without the permission of the coyright owner is unlawful. Requests for permission or further information should be addressed to: Cape Publications, Inc., 4838 Park Avenue, Bethesda, Maryland 20816; facsimile transmission number: (301) 229-3709.

Library of Congress Cataloging-in-Publication data

Ingersoll, Barbara D., 1945-; Betsy S. Davis, 1947-
        Your House at the Beach: Finding it, Buying it and Operating it.
Barbara D. Ingersoll and Betsy S. Davis - 1st ed.

        p. cm.

        "An identification of effective procedures, and problems to avoid, when buying and operating a beach house as a rental property."

        1. Real estate/beach — popular works.
        2. Vacation homes.

I. title.

ISBN # 0-9648548-1-3

10 9 8 7 6 5 4 3 2

Cover Photography by Bill Wood (Beach Home), Lynda Tanner (Sunset) and Ray Matthews (Sea and Sky)

CONTENTS

PREFACE

It happens to many people who vacation in rental "cottages" at the beach: they're relaxing on a deck or at a pool-side overlooking the ocean, soaking up the rays, when the thought occurs: "I'd love to have a place like this!"

The idea of living in a house overlooking the ocean is a compelling one for people all over the world. In fact, more than 2,000 years ago, wealthy Romans fled to their seaside villas to escape the summer heat — a strategic move that generations of people have emulated.

Some fortunate individuals can realize the dream of a seaside home, either through great wealth or because they work in professions which allow them to live close to the water.

For others, however — others, like us — the dream of a beach home can only be realized if we open our beach houses to a paying clientele who will occupy our homes during some or all of "the season" — the months of the year deemed most desirable to vacationers in that locale. How to go about finding, buying, and maintaining such a property is more complicated and fraught with more pitfalls than you might think. That, in a nutshell, is what this book is about.

As you read this book, you will note that we have identified some specific products by name. These are products we've discovered and tried in our own homes, with good results. There may be many more fine products other than those we've mentioned: we're just not aware of them.

We caution you, too, that our advice provides only broad guidelines. We do not pretend to be tax attorneys or investment advisors: discuss any legal and/or tax issues with your attorney or tax advisor.

ACKNOWLEDGMENTS

We are grateful to so many people who have provided us with valuable information about purchasing and operating a vacation rental home at the beach. Specifically, we wish to thank the following people for their contributions to this project. Essential information was provided by Greg Cremia, Paul Walk, James Barksdale, Mary Davenport, Matt Palmer and Craig Buckley.

The following real estate professionals from around the country are all associated with firms that are members of the Vacation Managers Rental Association (VRMA), and were kind enough to give us their time and advice: Barbara O'Brien, Brewster, MA; Coleen Susan, Brewster, MA; Jim Waggoner, Ocean City, MD; Peggy Welton, Virginia Beach, VA; Luanna Bowen, Topsail Beach, NC; Debbie Laney, Emerald Isle, NC; Peggy Kotnick, Emerald Isle, NC; Sue Muething, Surfside Beach, SC; Jane Oyler, St. Simon's Island, GA; Karen Poe, Destin, FL; Al Williams, Sanibel, FL; Wayne Gleason, St. George Island, FL; Jim Lord, Gulf Shores, AL; Janice Stohlman, Galveston, TX; Anne Reiswerg, Galveston, TX.

Special thanks are due to our "East Coast" reviewer, Barbara Leary of Twiddy & Company, Duck, NC and our "West Coast" reviewer, Jan Leasure, Monteray Bay Property Management, Monteray Bay, CA for reviewing the manuscript and ensuring that we were pointed in the right direction.

YOUR HOUSE AT THE BEACH:

FINDING IT, BUYING IT, AND OPERATING IT

CHAPTER ONE

THE BEACH HOUSE AS AN INVESTMENT

IS BEACH PROPERTY A GOOD INVESTMENT?

If you're looking to make a quick million, buying a beach house isn't the investment for you. In terms of a dollar-for-dollar return on your money, you could certainly expect a better return on your investment than you will realize through owning a beach house. In recent years, for example, the stock market has soared to unprecedented heights and some investors are making money hand over fist. Of course, bull markets have been known to crash and, unless you invest in government securities, there is no investment that is totally safe.

THE "PERKS"

It **is** safe, however, to say that few other investments offer the advantages that a vacation home can provide, especially as concerns quality-of-life — an asset on which it's impossible to place a dollar value. Owning a beach home means that you and your family can get away from the rat-race and head for a vacation spot where you know you'll be assured the comforts of home in a locale that delights you. In returning year after year to a familiar and well-loved beach, families develop their own rituals and traditions, along with a sense of belonging to the community.

Then, too, there is a certain cachet that comes with being an owner, instead of a renter. As an owner, you'll find that you feel more connected to the community and that you're considered a member of the beach community.   You may even be entitled to special sales and discounts offered only to owners. (After all, the merchants in beach communities depend on you, the property owner to bring them, via your tenants, their major source of income.) In fact, you might come to find the community so congenial that you'll want to retire there, as so many owners do.

Most people who own rental beach houses make greater use of their homes in the off-season than during the high season, when renters are willing to pay the prices that pay the mortgage on the house. But what you lose in accessability during the high season, you make up for many times over in other ways; that is, your ability to savor the joys of beach life without fighting the maddening crowds.
A scant decade or two ago, Labor Day brought about an abrupt end to activities at the beaches along the mid-Atlantic Coast. Stores and restaurants closed and the board-walk was virtually rolled up, along with all of its attractions. Now, however, with so many empty-nesters taking advantage of their freedom from school schedules, more beach communities are remaining open year 'round to cater to them. Even beaches along the northern Atlantic coast don't completely close during the winter: Acadia National Park on Maine's Mount Desert Island, for example, is open all year and even offers winter camping for truly hardy souls who come to admire the beauty of the winter beach.

And beaches in more temperate climes, such as those along the coast of the Carolinas, are particularly lovely during spring and fall. Even in the dead of winter, there are sunny days when beachgoers can stroll the beach barefoot, albeit wearing sweats instead of swimsuits.

On the West Coast and along the Gulf Coast, of course, vacationers can enjoy a holiday by the sea at any time during the year. In fact, more and more families are opting to spend traditional family holidays such as Thanksgiving and Christmas at the beach, especially if they own a home there. Many beach communities are especially festive during the Christmas season. On the East Coast, for example, Nantuckett's Christmas Stroll" is a community celebration in which Santa arrives via a Coast Guard vessel and rides up Main Street in a horse-drawn carriage. And on the West Coast, the story-book town of Carmel — lovely in any season — is at its most enchanting when decked with twinkling lights and holiday greens.

TAX ADVANTAGES

What follows is a brief overview of how vacation homes are treated for tax purposes under Section 280 of the Internal Revenue Code. Essentially, the IRS considers two broad categories: <u>type of residence</u> and <u>length of tenancy</u>.

TYPE OF RESIDENCE

Under current IRS regulations, your beach house can be classified in one of the following four categories.

> o **Personal Residence.** If your beach house is strictly for your personal use (unlikely if you are reading this book), the house is considered a second residence and you can deduct mortgage interest, real estate taxes, and casualty losses. If you rent your home for **fewer than 15 days a year,** the IRS will still consider the house to be a personal residence and you will not be taxed on the rent you receive, regardless of the amount. In fact, you don't even have to report this income.

> o **Personal Residence, Mixed Use.** The home is considered a residence subject to vacation home rules if it is rented for at least 15 days, and personal use **exceeds** the greater of 14 days or 10% of rental days.* Personal use is use by you, your family, friends, or others to whom you do not charge fair market rent. Note that this includes even "charitable contributions:" if, for example,

---

* A recent U.S. Tax Court of Appearls decision (M. Razavi, DA-6, No. 94-2193, 96-1 USTC, 50,060) may give the taxpayer additional relief in the 10% rule. In this case, the Court found that the entire 365-day lease period between the owner and the rental management company should prevail, regardless of the number of days the unit is actually rented. Thus, under the 10% rule, personal use would be 36.5 days.

you donate the use of your home for a week for charitable purposes, such as a fund-raiser for your child's private school, that week is counted towards your **personal** use. It is not considered a charitable contribution by the IRS, and you do not receive any tax break at all for your generosity.

Under IRS regulations, you can deduct property taxes, mortgage interest, and casualty losses. Rental income is then reduced by these deductions. The remaining income can be offset **but not exceeded by** depreciation and other operating expenses. These excess expenses can then be suspended, or carried forward, to future years.

o **Pure Rental Property**. If you rent your beach house without ever using it yourself or allowing friends and family to use it at less than fair market rent, it is considered a pure rental property. This means that the IRS will usually consider the house as Rental Real Estate Activity for purposes of the passive loss rule.

o **Rental Property, Mixed Use.** If your beach house is a rental property under IRS regulations, you can deduct all the expenses you would deduct with a personal residence. You can also deduct depreciation and other operating expenses, even if there is an overall rental loss, as there might be. The home falls under the same passive loss rules as a Pure Rental Property if it is rented for more than 14 days and personal use does not exceed 14 days, or 10 percent of the rental days, whichever is greater. Any rental loss will usually be covered by the rental and real estate passive loss rules that apply to a pure Rental Property.

The general rule for passive loss is this: **passive loses are deductible only to the extent that you have passive income from other sources.** Passive income is limited to income derived from a business in which you are not an active managing participant, or from rental property activity (unless you are a real estate professional). The exception to this rule allows you to deduct up to $25,000 ($12,500 for married, filing separately) of rental real estate losses, even if there is no passive income, provided that you meet the "active participation" test. Eligibility for this exception is phased out beginning with an adjusted gross income of $100,000 ($50,000 for married, filing separately).

LENGTH OF TENANCY

You must decide whether you will permit your beach house to be rented for less than a full week. You will want to consider your own personal tax situation before you make this decision because it can affect whether the IRS considers your property to be a Business or a Rental Real Estate Activity.

> o **Business.** If your average rental period is 7 days or less, the IRS considers your vacation home to be a business, much like a hotel. This business can still be a passive activity, subject to the passive activity rules discussed above, but you will not qualify for the $25,000 deduction exception unless you meet the active participation test. To meet this test, you must show that you actively participate in the management of the rental property (e.g. by advertising, selecting tenants, and the like). It is almost impossible to show active participation if you employ a property management firm, since significant hands-on involvement is necessary to pass the test. If you **can** show that you actively participate, any rental loss is then non-passive and can be deducted against non-passive income up to the $25,000 maximum, as determined by your Adjusted Gross Income.

In other words:

> 1) If you rent an average of 7 days or less, you are not eligible for the $25,000 deduction exception — period.
>
> 2) If you rent an average of 7 days or less and do not actively participate in the management of the rental property, any loss is passive and can only be deducted against passive income.
>
> 3) If you rent an average of 7 days or less and **do** actively participate in the management of the rental property, any loss is non-passive and can be deducted against non-passive income.
>
> o **Real Estate Rental Activity**. If your average rental period is more than 7 days, the IRS considers you to have a Real Estate Rental Activity, rather than a business. Therefore, any rental loss is subject to the $25,000 deduction exception, provided that you

meet the active participation rules. In order for your average rental period to exceed 7 days, all you need is **one rental per year** that is longer than 7 days and **no** rentals for fewer than 7 days.

You can see why it is important to review your tax situation with your accountant or tax attorney to determine whether short-term or long-term rental is better for you. Many factors — including your Adjusted Gross Income, whether you have other sources of passive income, and whether you actively participate in managing the rental property — will affect your decision.

The IRS may not be the only government entity interested in your length of tenancy decisions. The city of Carmel-by-the-Sea in California passed an ordinace prohibiting rentals of fewer than 30 days in homes located in residential areas. After nearly a decade, the city's right to enact such limitations has been upheld by the courts under its "zoning authority," an extension of its police powers. Opponents claimed Carmel's intent was to discriminate against tenants who couldn't afford a full month's vacation and rent. The city countered that it was merely trying to preserve the character of its residential areas and limited tenancy of less than 30 days to buildings (hotels, Bed-and-Breakfast houses, etc.) located in areas that were zoned for commercial use. Several communities on both coasts are considering similar zoning regulations: check before you buy!

RECORD KEEPING

As we noted previously, your beach house will be considered a rental property under IRS regulations only if your personal use of the home is limited to 14 days per year or 10 percent of the number of days the house is rented, whichever is greater. Thus, if your home is rented for 200 days a year, you are limited to 20 days of personal use — that is, use by your family, friends, and others to whom you do not charge fair market rent.

It's important to note, however, that days spent at your beach house doing cleaning, maintenance, and repairs are not calculated as personal use days. This means that your family can enjoy frolicking on the beach while you paint, polish, and putty. Just be sure to keep good records for the IRS.

For this, we suggest a simple spiral-bound notebook used as a job-log. Make a list of the chores you plan to accomplish and, as each task is completed, enter the date — or dates, if it's a more complicated project that requires several days — on which the chore was accomplished. It makes sense, too, to leave a "paper trail" in the form of receipts from local stores where you purchase building materials and cleaning supplies. Such a trail is additional evidence that you did more than simply enjoy the sea air during your maintenance days.

You should seriously consider opening accounts at the local hardware store, paint store, and so forth. This gives you the opportunity to get to know the local merchants, most of whom can give you good advice about which of their products work best in a beach environment. They are also valuable sources of information about other service providers in the neighborhood. Many local merchants also extend discounts on merchandise and services to property owners: ask your property manager if their firm has negotiated such discounts with local merchants.

For convenience in keeping records, you might also designate one major credit card as your beach charge card. Apart from purchases made at beach stores where you have an account, charge all purchases to that card only, whether the merchandise is bought at the beach or elsewhere. This will save you countless hours of rooting through receipts and credit-card ledgers at tax time. In addition, the fees charged by the credit card company may be deductible as a business expense.

Of course, you should also open a separate checking account for paying bills associated with the house. It is to this account that all rent receipts should be deposited.

APPRECIATION

If you were smart enough, or lucky enough, to have bought an ocean-front lot in Avon in North Carolina's Outer Banks in the early '70's, as friends of ours did, you would have paid about $15,000. That lot is now worth anywhere from $150,000 to $175,000. If you had spent $20,000 to build a cottage on the lot, your rental income would have paid off the mortgage in ten years and you would have owned the property outright. You could then have re-financed, refurbished the cottage, and paid off that mortgage in ten years, again using only rental income. Had you done that, you would now own a lot worth $150-175,000 and a mortgage-free cottage. If, like our friends, you were able to find a buyer who would purchase your home and move it to another site (because beach houses are often built on pilings, they are amazingly "portable"), you would be in a great position to build the house of your dreams on your paid-for lot and start all over again in even grander style.

Ocean-side lots — that is, lots that are on the ocean side of the highway but do not front directly on the beach — appreciate less rapidly than ocean-front properties. However, they do appreciate: if, for example, you had bought an ocean-side lot on the Outer Banks for $12,000 in the mid-1970's, that lot would now be worth $55,000 to $65,000.

In Florida, the demand for water-front homes has pushed prices up considerably in recent years. While it was rare to pay as much as $200 per square foot of waterfront property in the 1980's, buyers are now paying $275. And, in luxury projects in Miami Beach and Boca Ratan, costs are more than $400 per square foot!

And this may be only a portent of things to come. Wallace Epperson, a Richmond, Virginia investment banker who studies national real estate demographic trends, predicts that more vacation homes will by purchased by aging "baby boomers," in part because inheritances are coming later in life, after college tuitions and mortgages have been paid off. In fact, $16 trillion in inheritances is expected between now and the year 2010.

What will the boomers do with all that money? You guessed it: they will buy second homes for vacations and eventual retirement. In fact, studies such as those conducted by the American Resort Development Association in 1995 show that more people now than ever before are considering buying a vacation home. Among these people, the first choice for a vacation home is a house at the beach. According to the U.S. Census Bureau, coastal areas represent 46 percent of new residential construction and 65 percent of total building permits (new construction and additions) in this country.[*] No wonder Florida is booming!

---

[*] There's even a magazine, *Coastal Living*, devoted to the interests of this group -- "people who live or vacation on the coast . . . and those who dream of such a thing." To subscribe to this enjoyable and informative magazine, call 1-888-252-3529

But, in spite of the fact that more people now than ever before want homes at the beach, there is only a limited amount of beach property available. Thus, the law of supply and demand dictates that property values at the beach will continue to increase.

CAPITAL GAINS

Under the recent changes in the capital gains taxes that apply to a principal residence, homeowners will be able to exclude up to $500,000 in gains from **each** sale of a principal residence (single taxpayers could exclude up to $250,000 in gains), without limitation. To qualify as a principal residence, the owner must live in the home for two of the last five years. This means that you can sell your current home, take up to $500,000 in profit tax-free, buy another home, live in it for two of the last five years and sell it, also taking up to $500,000 in profit tax-free. And you can continue this process ad infinitum.

Capital gains from the sale of a vacation home are treated differently, however. Assuming you have never rented your beach house, if you sold it today you would pay capital gains taxes at the 20 percent capital gains tax rate. But there is a way to avoid your tax liability, as the following example indicates:

> **EXAMPLE:** John and Brenda Jones live in their principal residence for 20 years, then sell it at a profit of $300,000. Under the new tax law, this profit is tax free. They then retire to the beach home they have owned and rented-out for six years and live there for two years or longer. When they sell that home, at a profit of $250,000, this profit is also tax free.

How are your gains treated if you have used your beach house as rental property? You will have to comply with the new depreciation "recapture" rules that expose you to a portion of the gain when you sell. In this situation, you could reduce your tax liability by converting the beach house to your principal residence and taking your existing tax basis as your measuring point for computing gain.

> **EXAMPLE:** John and Brenda buy a beach house for $100,000 and take $20,000 in depreciation deductions over the years they operate it as a rental property. Their tax basis is $80,000 ($100,000 minus the $20,000 in depreciation). They sell their principal residence and move into the beach house. After two or more years, they sell the beach house for $300,000. Given their basis of $80,000, they now have a gain of $220,000. John and Brenda must divide their gain into two parts: the gain attributed to the depreciation they took will be taxed at the "recapture" rate of 25 percent while the remainder of their gain qualifies as profit from the sale of a principal residence and is tax free.

A word of caution is in order about changing your beach house to your principal residence. In order to convince the IRS that your beach house is really your principal residence, you must actually live in the house and do all of the things you would normally do when changing residences, i.e. change your driver's license, your car registration, and your voter registration. Don't try to scam Uncle Sam!

DEPRECIATION

Under the U.S. Tax Code, you can write off business purchases, up to a certain point, in the year in which the expense is incurred. For large purchases with long life-spans, the purchase must be "depreciated" over several years. The number of years over which property, equipment, and improvements can be depreciated depends on the expected life of the item itself.

Thus a beach house must be depreciated over 39 years, since this is the useful life of real estate under IRS regulations. Substantial improvements to the structure (e.g.: adding a room) also fall under the 39 year rule. The cost of repairs and maintenance, however, can be deducted fully in the year in which you incur their costs. Caution: if you make too many otherwise deductable repairs in the same year, the IRS may insist that you are engaging in a "general pattern of improvements" and force you to apply the 39 year depreciation.

Usually, business furniture and moveable equipment requires a 7 year depreciation, but for a rental property (in which all of the contents of the house are used by your tenents), the depreciation time-frame is reduced to 5 years. Check with your tax advisor for specifics on using the "bonus depreciation allowance" and the fastest write-off methods for assets which fall into different useful-life categories.

Remember, as noted above, you will have to pay a 25 percent "recapture" tax on the depreciation you have taken when you sell your beach house.

THE ECONOMICS OF RENTAL PROPERTY

Will your beach house pay for itself? That depends on a number of factors. What kind of mortgage will you take out, for example? How many weeks each year will your house be available for rent? What are your costs, in comparison to the rental income you can reasonably expect?

Some home owners limit rentals to the high season, while others open the house to rentals during off-season as well. Still others place their homes in the rental market year 'round. It is this last group — the year 'rounders — who stand the best chance of not only meeting expenses, but of actually winding up with a tidy profit at the end of the year.

Of course, so much depends on the size of your mortgage. If you are able to put down 40-50 percent of the purchase price, you can expect to break even or turn a profit.

> **EXAMPLE:** Ted and Terry purchased a furnished ocean-front home for $600,000. Their down payment was $300,000 and they carry a 15-year mortgage at 7-3/4 percent. Their rental income of $64,000 was more than enough to offset expenses of $58,250, leaving them with a profit of $5,260.

Note, however, that if Ted and Terry had put down 40 percent, they would be in the red to the tune of $5,000. Note, too, that annual return on investment is greater if the mortgage is financed over 20 years instead of 15: if Ted and Terry put a 50 percent down-payment, their profit for the year is $9,560; if they had put a 40 percent down-payment, their profit would be $3,690. But, think about it: do you really want to finance your investment property for 20 years? Remember that the average length of home ownership for beach property is ten years.

Of course, Ted and Terry could make their house available for rent throughout the year, in the hope of increasing rental income. If their beach house is in an area where winters are mild, they might pick up an additional $5,000-10,000 in rental income.

Some developers who also offer financing advertise a deal that consists of a 20 percent down-payment "and your house will pay for itself." We advise caution here, since we have heard horror stories of owners forced into bankruptcy because they could not handle such large mortgages.

In real estate, the rule of thumb is to expect at least a 10 percent annual return on your investment. Beach properties are a bit different, however: as we've noted, the enjoyment you gain from your beach house may compensate you for accepting a smaller return on your investment.

EXPENSES

The expenses for your beach house consist of your initial outlay and your ongoing expenses, such as property management fees, maintenance, and utilities.

INITIAL OUTLAY. After closing on the home itself, your initial expenses will vary according to whether you have bought or built. As we discuss in Chapter 4, if you build a home, you will have to furnish it in one fell swoop. While actual costs can vary enormously, depending on the size of the house and the quality of the furnishings you select, the expense will be significant.

On the other hand, your maintenance and repair costs during the first several years will be relatively low, since the plumbing, the wiring, the roof, the appliances, and so forth will be new and covered by warranty.

If you buy an existing house already furnished, your initial expenses after closing will be determined by the condition of the structure, the appliances, and the furnishings. Take careful stock of the condition of the house and contents, using the inspection report as a guide and be sure to budget for replacements and repairs.

MAINTENANCE AND UTILITIES. Expect to pay higher utility bills for your beach house than for your principal residence. This is because some of your paying guests think nothing of leaving doors and windows open while operating the air conditioning at full blast. (And, for some strange reason, they will also set the thermostat 10 degrees cooler at **your** house than at **their** house.) It also takes a lot of current to keep those hot tubs and pool pumps going. The end result: expect electric bills that are higher than you think they might be.

Your water bills, too, may be higher than you anticipate because pools, hot tubs, and jacuzzi tubs use a lot of water. Then, too, there's the occasional tenant who forgets to turn off the hose after sluicing down his car or his feet.

Unfortunately, there's little you can do to keep these costs down. Installing water-saving shower heads, for example, won't really save much water in comparison with the amount of water used for pools and hot tubs and will only serve to aggravate your guests and make you look cheap. The same can be said for the strategy of pre-setting and locking the thermostat for the air conditioner.

Maintenance costs will also be higher at the beach. Little things, such as the door that sticks ever-so-slightly and the bathtub that drains a bit slowly, will result in calls to your property management company. These calls, in turn, will result in repair costs billed to your account. You can help keep these costs in check by conducting regular maintenance inspections or arranging with your property management firm to do so as part of the cleaning service.

PROPERTY MANAGEMENT FEES. Property management fees can range from a low of 15% of the weekly rental income to a high of 60%, depending on the locale, the type of property (private house versus condo), and the services included in the property management fee. In some upscale resort communities, for example, property management services include not only advertising to prospective renters and making reservations, but cleaning services, maintenance, and linen service as well. Obviously, the property management fee will be much higher than in communities in which only basic services such as reservations and rent collection are provided. We will discuss this subject in greater detail in Chapter 5.

MISCELLANEOUS EXPENSES.   Many neighborhoods at the beach have neighborhood associations that property owners are required to join, usually at an annual fee of $200-300. These associations lobby the local governing body concerning zoning ordinances, roads, and water and sewer availability. They also establish neighborhood watch programs and may set restrictive covenants for the neighborhood.

INCOME

Your property management company has experts who can help you determine an appropriate rate schedule for in-season, mid-season, and out-of-season rentals. They can also give you valuable tips on maximizing your rental income: they know, for example, what amenities are most likely to attract renters in your locale and can advise you about making your home competitive with others in the area.

It's a good idea, too, to peruse rental brochures from other management companies on the beach to compare the rent for properties similar to yours. These brochures can also be a source of good ideas for up-grading your own beach house when the time comes to do so. In fact, you might even take the time to visit other vacation rental properties in your locale and price range. See for yourself what amenities these properties have so you can judge your competition accordingly.

CHAPTER TWO

FINDING YOUR DREAM HOUSE

DO YOUR HOMEWORK

If you are considering buying a beach house, you have almost certainly located the area in which you would like to own a vacation home. Maybe it's a beach resort you have visited and enjoyed many times over the years. Or maybe it's a love-at-first-sight experience: you enjoy a week at a lovely beach and suddenly no other vacation spot looks nearly as appealing.

In any case, there is no substitute for in-depth knowledge of real estate values in the area of your choice. Before you even consider purchasing a vacation home, you should visit as many homes in your price range as you possibly can. In this way, you will get a sense of property values in the area and you can begin to get a feel for what constitutes a good deal and a sound investment.

You also want to learn as much about the general area as you can. Is this a well-established resort area to which families return year after year?

Or is it an up-and-coming area which offers a promising return on invest-ment to those investors who have the foresight to buy in early in the game?

What kind of vacation homes exist in the area? What is the rental income they produce? Is the home you are considering buying or building con-sistent with surrounding properties? Remember, you don't want to own a high-priced property in an area surrounded by low-priced properties unless you have very good reason to believe that the area is slated for up-scale redevelopment in the near future.

WORKING WITH A REAL ESTATE AGENT

When an individual, (the seller) lists his property for sale with a real estate professional, that agent and his firm must then work to obtain the best price and terms for the seller, since they are employed by him to do so. Whether he is a builder or a current owner, he probably has an advan-tage over you: he knows the area and the real estate market, and has hired a top-notch professional to represent him. How do you find one just as good?

As with everything we've said so far in this chapter, there is no substitute for doing your homework. Remember: unless other arrangements are made that are acceptable to all parties, the agent you select to represent you will be paid by commission from the sale — in effect, the seller pays. We recommend that you use the information in this section when select-ing and working with a real estate professional, and there are some gen-eral guidelines you should keep in mind.

If you already have your eye on a particular house that is for sale, you probably don't want to contact the real estate company whose sign is on the property, since that company is already committed to getting the best deal for the seller. If you do go with the same company, you will have to sign an agreement of "dual agency," specifically recognizing that the company represents both you and the seller. The result: you do not have someone who is working exclusively in your best interest. In fact, it is in the company's best interest to work to reach a "deal" — to close the sale.

Therefore, whether you have already selected you dream house, or are starting from scratch, we recommend that you select an agent who will provide the services we outline below. Indeed, with an eye toward delivering those services in the buyer's best interest, the real estate industry has developed the concept of a **buyer's agent** or **buyer's broker**.

These agents and firms advertise specifically that they will represent the best interest of the buyer. Any real estate professional can be your buyer's agent, so long as he truly represents your best interests and works to obtain the best price and terms for you. You, not "the deal," are the number one priority.

Although a buyer's agent is usually associated with one firm, he probably has access to every property on the market, regardless of which agency has listed the property for sale. If the agent and his firm also have homes for sale, you can even insist that he not show you any of "their" listings, in order to avoid the problem of dual agency that we noted above. In fact, in some highly competitive real estate markets, especially in expensive urban areas, some firms have evolved that never represent sellers or list any houses for sale at all — they only serve buyers.[*]   Real estate professionals in most beach communities, however, cannot afford to set themselves up this way: the market is just too confined.

In short: it doesn't matter whether the real estate professional you select calls himself a buyer's agent or not, so long as he acts like one.

SELECTING AN AGENT

Since you will be working very closely with the agent you select, it is absolutely vital that you have confidence in him and that you are comfortable working in partnership with him. And a partnership it is: you will have to rely on your agent for many things, particularly if you do not live in the immediate geographic area. For this reason, we suggest that

---

* In these same markets, buyer's agents may be willing to negotiate terms that actually result in a portion of their seller-paid commission being turned-over to the buyer (if, for example they agree to work on a time and materials contract). In general, however, agents in beach communities don't negotiate such contracts.

you interview two or three agents from different real estate firms to compare services offered and to assess your comfort level with each agent.
You are about to enter into a long and complicated process that could be
both uncomfortable and unproductive if you work with an agent in whom
you don't have full confidence.

What should you look for in an agent? First, we suggest that you select
an agent who works full-time in real estate. Some part-time agents are
not active enough in the business to be fully familiar with the market or
to stay on top of a prospective deal for you. You also want an agent who
is familiar with general market trends in your area: as a prospective
owner, you want to know what's hot and what's not, in terms of attract-
ing prospective tenants. And, of course, you want to work with a successful agent, so be sure to ask how many properties he or she has closed
on within the past year.

It's important, too, that an agent be responsive to you. How long does it
take him to return your calls, for example? Does he or she sound as har-
ried as you feel or come across as calm and in control?

WHAT TO EXPECT FROM YOUR AGENT

Before your agent can provide you with helpful information, he or she
must first determine your specific needs and wants. As one successful
agent succinctly explained: "Sometimes what you want is not available
and what you need is different from what you want. Everybody **wants**
ocean-front; most find that ocean-side is what they **need** — and can
afford."

After you and your agent have determined your wants and your needs,
what then?   At a **minimum**, your agent should provide you with the following information:

> o A list of all available properties that meet your stated require-
> ments, with maps or directions to each;
>
> o Sales information about comparable properties ("comps") sold
> within the past two years;

o Rental history for each property;

o Shore-line annual erosion rates for the past ten years (an East Coast, not a West Coast problem);

o Tax rates;

o Any plans he is aware of that involve developing adjacent property;

o Any local, state or federal plans that could affect your property.

A **thorough** agent will also provide the following information:

o A list of attorneys who specialize in real estate closings (if an attorney is required — they are, mercifully, unnecesarry in some States);

o A list of insurance companies;

o A list of home inspectors;

o A list of mortgage companies and lending institutions;

o Addresses and telephone numbers of utility companies.

An **excellent** agent will also provide the following services:

o Obtain quotes from attorneys regarding closing fees;

o Open utility and telephone accounts for you;

o Monitor the construction process if you choose to build;

o Ensure that all appropriate inspections are completed;

o Keep you fully informed at every step of the way.

Finding your special "place in the sun" and then negotiating the deal and closing the deal is an arduous and draining process under the best of circumstances. **A good buyer's agent can make the entire process much less painful. Our advice: do yourself a favor and get one!**

YOUR DREAM HOUSE: SHOULD YOU BUY OR BUILD?

BUYING YOUR BEACH HOUSE

One of us was lucky enough to fall into a dream of a deal — a beautifully furnished beach-front home with all of the amenities — right down to lovely sheets, towels, and a fully-stocked bar. And, best of all, the price made it a very good deal. Bear in mind, however, that even with a spouse who is a real-estate professional, we looked for years in the area of our choice before finding the perfect house. Over those years, we walked through countless moldy, down-at-the-heels, overpriced houses that neither of us would have wanted to spend a night in, much less own and manage.

But we were in no hurry. When our dream house came on the market at such a reasonable price, it took us less than ten minutes to make the decision to buy. We knew the market, we knew the area, we knew the realtor, so we were ready to pounce — and we've never been sorry.

Don't expect to find your dream house on your first outing — or even your tenth. Instead, be prepared for a search before you find the house that's just right for your needs and your budget. If you buy rather than build, it may take a bit more legwork and patience than you expect.

Many, if not most, beach houses on the re-sale market are sold furnished, as ours was. If you like the former owner's taste, this relieves you of the burden of selecting and purchasing an entire houseful of furniture, accessories, kitchen ware, and the like. All you may need to make the house your very own is your toothbrush!

There's an additional advantage to buying: if the house you purchase has previously been in a rental program, you may find that it comes with a loyal following of repeat renters. This means that you will enter your first rental season with at least part of your income assured for the season.

Home Inspection. Don't even think about buying a beach house without first obtaining a home inspection from a qualified inspector. In fact, write the need for such an inspection into your contract of sale and ask your agent to steer you to a home inspector who is knowledgeable, thorough, and even a bit on the compulsive side.

A competent home inspector will be aware of the special demands placed on rental homes at the beach as well as the particular toll taken on homes in a beach environment. On the basis of this knowledge, he might, for example, recommend installing extra rails under benches on the deck to prevent a small child from falling through the aperture. Because he knows the havoc that a marine environment can wreak upon every nut and bolt in a structure, you can use his report to guide your own maintenance and repair plans for at least the first few years during which you own the home.

If there are structural problems that are likely to cost you money in repair bills in the near future, you should obtain an estimate of repair costs from a reputable builder in the area. This estimate can serve as a valuable bargaining tool in negotiating the cost of the property.

BUILDING YOUR BEACH HOUSE

If you decide to build, you should know that building your dream house from scratch — or even purchasing a "spec" house which is already under construction — is no easy matter, as one of us discovered the hard way. In fact, as we shall explain, building and furnishing a beach house is an undertaking that demands the utmost in stamina, patience, and attention to detail — an effort unlike that which you have ever put forth, even if you have designed and built your own home in the past.

If you have had previous experience in building a house from the ground up, you know that the experience is nerve-wracking and fraught with major and minor disasters from start to finish. Simply selecting a plan is difficult enough: very few people have the ability to visualize three-dimensional space from an architect's blueprint, no matter how detailed the blueprint.

After you select the plan, you must still spend long hours selecting the materials and fixtures from a bewildering array of products and price ranges. (Do you have any idea how many colors and styles toilets come in? You're about to find out!)

Once construction is underway, you will want to visit the building site as often as you can to be sure that everything is being done according to the plan. Otherwise, the poplar wainscoting you stipulated in the plan may be mysteriously replaced by pine and the lights that were supposed to be hung at eye level might wind up near the ceiling. If you live too far away, it might not be possible to check on progress in person. In this case, you might want to take Tom Philbin's[*] suggestion and hire a professional home inspector to help supervise the job by making several visits during the construction process. Of course, this service isn't free but it is a wise way to protect your investment, particularly since the contractor is apt to be less inclined to cut corners if he knows that his work is being inspected by an objective professional.

In any case, multiply all of the work cited above by a factor of ten if you live far away from the building site and you can begin to appreciate what a challenge it is to build a beach house! We can assure you, too, that watching your house come down to the wire as the rental season approaches is truly a hair-raising experience.

Advantages to Building. Of course, there are advantages to building or buying a house under construction instead of buying one already built. An obvious advantage is that you can customize the house to meet your own needs and tastes. You can, for example, include generous-sized "owner's closets" in which to lock away your clothing, linens, liquor and non-perishable foods, and other personal gear you don't choose to share with your tenants. (Note: since many tenants are insatiably curious, use a dead-bolt lock to safeguard the contents of your owner's closets from their curiosity.)

---

[*] *How to Hire a Home Improvement Contractor without Getting Chiseled.* New York: St. Martin's Press, 1996.

You can also include some unusual but highly desirable features such as two dishwashers, extra refrigerators, and ice-makers (nice in any home — necessary in larger homes that sleep more than 15). For a source of ideas, visit some of the high-end model homes in your resort area.

If you build, you have the opportunity to select the most maintenance-free products and materials, such as the following:

o Exterior siding such as **HardiPlank** (manufactured by James Hardie, 1-800-9-HARDIE). This product, a composite of cement, sand, and cellulose fiber, resists salt-spray and wind-driven sand. It also stands up well in gale-force winds.

o Decking of wood-polymer lumber, such as **Trex** (1-800-BUY TREX or www.trex.com.). Comparable to treated wood in cost and in installation costs: it resists rot and insects and needs no stains or sealants for protection, although it can be painted or stained just like wood. The company offers a limited 10-year warranty against splintering, splitting, checking, rot, decay, and termite damage.

o A "knock-down" finish on the walls. This is a rough-textured surface that tends to hide minor blemishes.

o Latex enamel paint in areas subject to splashes from grease and water.

o Exterior doors of wood or fiberglass. Avoid steel doors which are quickly reduced to rusted skeletons in a beach environment.

o Casement windows which can be securely latched against wind-driven rain from hurricanes and storms. Avoid double-hung windows which are prone to leak under these conditions. Builders agree that aluminum-clad or vinyl-clad wood is the best choice because they combine the beauty of wood on the inside with a maintenance-free exterior.

o <u>Shades on windows and doors that operate between the panes of glass, protecting them from dust, dirt, and damage.</u> On such doors and windows from **Pella**, for example, the inside panel is easily removed when you want to change the style or color of the shades.

o <u>Durable screens on windows and doors.</u> Fiberglass is a good option in terms of price and resistance to corrosion. On screen doors, reinforce the bottom area of the screen by adding wood or metal supports to avoid the bulging-bottom syndrome.

o <u>Low-maintenance light fixtures.</u> Select fixtures of opaque glass and/or those which are constructed so that the entire assembly can be easily removed in one piece for cleaning.

o <u>Built-in vacuum-cleaner or one on each floor.</u> If the vacuum cleaner is readily accessible, your guests are likely to use it more often, thereby prolonging the life of your floors.

o <u>Flooring material that will stand up well under the pitter-patter of many sandy feet.</u> Hardwood floors will not, but the newer laminates will. These laminates consist of a wear-resistant laminate over a decorative layer (stone, marble, or wood patterns) that is then bonded to a wood-based core. The laminate surface is further strengthened by hard particles, making it about 25 times stronger than the laminate of a kitchen countertop, so the surface is highly resistant to stains, burns, and other mishaps. **Pergo,** for example, guarantees their flooring for 15 years against wear, stains, and fading; **Witex** guarantees theirs for ten years.[*] Plan to spend about $65 per square yard, installed, for a laminate floor.

---

[*] It's important to note that manufacturer's warranties apply **only** to products used in an owner-occupied house. Thus, while warranties are useful for the purpose of comparison shopping, they may not be honored in a rental home unless you purchase a commercial grade. This is true of appliances, as well.

Ceramic tile is the most durable of floor coverings and may well outlast your ownership of the house. At somewhere between $70 and $90 per square yard installed, a ceramic-tile floor will resist almost anything but a bowling-ball dropped on it. And should a tenant drop such a bowling-ball, the cracked tile can be replaced. In high-traffic areas such as kitchens, ceramic tile will not only outperform vinyl (about $34 per square yard; life- expectancy of 8 to 10 years); it also looks much richer.

If you don't like the gritty feel of inevitable sand tracked across floors, use a good grade of nylon carpet, treated to resist stains. **Wear-Dated** (TM) by Montsanto or **Stainmaster** (TM) by DuPont are good choices. For best wear, our experts recommend a 40-ounce synthetic felt pad or a six-pound re-bond pad. Solid foam, which is a bit more expensive, is also a good choice. For carpet, plan to spend about $24 per square yard and expect it to last for 8 to 10 years unless it is subjected to abuse such as burns or cutting.

If you build, you can also take advantage of the latest in technology to make your house as weather-proof and guest-proof as possible. You might, for example, install sensors attached to all exterior doors: if a door is left open for more than five minutes, the air-conditioner shuts down and cannot be turned on again until the door is closed.

If you build, remember that building codes set **minimum** standards. There are many additional steps you can take to help your beach house survive the onslaught of severe storms. For example, most experienced beach contractors recommend the use of 2x6 exterior walls and 5/8-inch sheathing. They also recommend that wood components be glued as well as nailed and that more nails be used in attaching sheathing and flooring to the frame than the number required by code.

For those building at the beach, a wealth of information about construction materials and designs most suited to withstand the demands of a beach environment — hurricanes and all — is available from Blue Sky, an organization that offers information about hazard-resistant home designs, construction methods, and materials. Many of their suggestions can be used, too, when the time comes to make renovations to an existing home. You can call for information (1-888-6-BLUE SKY) or check their web-site (WWW.BLUESKY-PROJECT.COM).

Finding A Contractor.   Because beach conditions are so different from conditions inland, beach construction must be different, too, if the house is to withstand the onslaught of winds and weather conditions unique to a water-side setting. This means that, before all else, your contractor should be someone who has had considerable experience in building beach houses in your chosen locale. Never, ever consider buying a house built by a contractor who lacks such specific experience! Otherwise, you are likely to wind up with a house which may be beautiful but not well able to withstand the demands of a beach environment.

How should you go about finding the right contractor to build your vacation home on the shore? This is really a million-dollar question, since you will have a big investment riding on your contractor's ability to produce a top-quality product in a timely manner.

Beach communities — even big, bustling beach communities — are really like small towns: everybody knows a lot about everybody else's business. Therefore, the first step in finding a good contractor is to **talk** with people.

> o Talk with real estate professionals. Since beach real estate firms usually offer property management services in addition to sales, they are in a good position to know which local contractors' houses hold up well and who produces houses in frequent need of repair. As sales agents, they can also tell you which contractors are likely to meet deadlines and those who don't.

> o Talk with local building inspectors. They can offer an expert's perspective on local contractors — which ones produce a solid product and which ones are likely to cut too many corners.

> o Talk with clients for whom contractors on your list have built homes. Ask if they would select the same contractor to build another house for them. Ask, too, about any problems they might have had with the contractor. You should also visit a few of the contractor's most recent projects (easily done during off-season when most houses are vacant) to inspect the work for yourself.

o Talk with the contractor. Find out how long he has been in business: the building business is a tough one and many who aren't "up to snuff" don't last very long. Ask, too, if he is licensed or registered. Although licensing does not guarantee competence, it tells you that the contractor at least paid a fee and proved that he had liability insurance in order to become licensed or registered.

o Finally, check with the consumer protection office or the Better Business Bureau in the local area to find out whether the contractor has had complaints lodged against him. Again, to paraphrase Tom Philbin, this won't tell you everything (sometimes complaints are unfounded) but it helps eliminate obvious bad actors. Real estate agents, too, are a good source of information: do the homes built by a particular builder bring better re-sale prices?

Monitoring the Progress. If you need to maximize your rental income, as most of us do, your house must be ready to receive guests by the beginning of "the season." Depending on the size of the house, the contractor will tell you that it will take between five and six months to complete: plan on seven to eight months.

Then plan on spending a lot of time and effort to ensure that your house will be ready by the drop-dead date. Remember, everyone else who is building and furnishing a beach house that season wants his home completed in time for the rental season, too.

Be sure to allow enough time for your personal use of the house prior to the arrival of your first paying guests. This will give you an opportunity to experience your house as your tenants will experience it and to spot and correct problems such as leaky plumbing, cranky appliances, and other glitches before your guests arrive.

This is a good time, too, to take a careful inventory of the contents of your home, something you will need to do so that the member of the property-management staff assigned to inspect your home for damage after each set of tenants departs will have a document to which to refer. You will also need such an inventory for insurance purposes in the event of a fire, flood, burglary, or other calamity. Your property management firm can provide you with a form to inventory the contents of your house.

For your own protection against fire, theft, vandalism, flood, storm damage, negligence, the I.R.S. and other natural and man-made disasters, we urge you to take a complete inventory of your beach home's contents.

Whether you buy new and furnish it from the ground up, or purchase an existing home that is already furnished, you want to know the true market value of this portion of your investment.

In some beach communities, when a house is sold fully furnished, the actual value of the contents may be considerably undervalued at the time of closing. This can result, for example, from a mortgage bank appraisal aimed at verifying the value of the property, because such an appraisal is not permitted to take contents into consideration. In this case, you should obtain an independent appraisal of the fair market value of the contents, so that you can justify your request to the insurance company for a higher value on your furnishings than might otherwise be permitted by the insurer. Of course, all acquired contents would be listed with the same date of purchase and a lump-sum value. Only those furnishings you add subsequent to purchase need to be reflected in an inventory. In short, however, an inventory is important for many reasons: take the time to protect yourself!

THE CONDOMINIUM ALTERNATIVE

Another popular option for home ownership at the beach is the condominium. In fact, in some beach resort areas, condos greatly outnumber single-family homes. Their popularity derives from a combination of lower cost than single-family homes along with freedom from maintenance headaches.

Condos vary as much as single-family homes in terms of style, size, and cost. Depending on the complex, the location, and the size of the unit, condo prices range from below $75,000 to well over $1 million in posh resort areas. At Porto Vita in Aventura, Florida, two tower suites recently listed at $2.35 million apiece. Condominium complexes vary greatly, too: a complex may have as few as twelve units with one communal pool or it may have hundreds of units, spread out over large areas. There are even condos within hotels: in Myrtle Beach, South Carolina, for example, some hotels have sold "efficiency apartments" (one room with bath and kitchenette) to private owners who place them on the vacation rental market as condos.

Many condominium associations employ management companies to maintain the grounds and to handle maintenance and repairs. The management company may also have a rental agency on the premises which can handle the management of your condo for you. Or, if you prefer, you can employ an independent company of your choice to do this.

THE NUTS AND BOLTS OF CONDO OWNERSHIP

When you purchase a condo, what are you really buying? In a condominium, you own the interior of your unit. You are a joint owner, along with all of the other owners in the condo association, of the exterior walls of the structure and the so-called "common areas;" that is, hallways, walkways, elevators, parking lots, pools, and so on. In general, the rule is that if it serves your condo only, you own it; if it serves more than one owner, it is the property of the condo association (i.e. common area).

A condominium complex usually has an owners' association comprised of all of the owners and governed by a board of directors. The governing document of the association, known as the "declaration," is formulated by the developer of the condominium prior to the sale of any units. The declaration, which is governed by state law, generally contains a description of common elements, limited elements, and units (e.g. are windows and balconies part of individual units or limited common elements). It also spells out the responsibilities of the owners of individual condos and the association and prevents individual owners from making major external changes or internal structural changes in the complex. Amending the declaration may be quite difficult: in many cases, the declaration can only be amended by a vote of 100 per cent of the members.

Condominum associations also have by-laws which govern the day-to-day operations of the association, such as how the board of directors is made up, how the property is maintained, and restrictions on use of units. When problems arise, the by-laws are not always clear as to how the problem should be resolved. If, for example, your bathtub overflows and the water damages the ceiling in the condo beneath yours, who is responsible for the repairs: you? the other condo owner? the association? In 1985, North Carolina passed a law mandating that declarations be written more clearly and placing more responsibility on the condo association but many grey areas such as this still exist.

On the other hand, a condo association usually has buying power that you, as an individual owner, do not have. For example, one association in Emerald Isle, North Carolina, wanted cable television. Since the association voted to require that every owner participate, the association was able to obtain cable at a cost of $9.18 per month, as opposed to the regular rate of $33.50.

Fees.   Condo owners must pay monthly dues to the condominium association. This fee is based on the size of the unit, generally calculated by numer of bedrooms in the unit. The fee covers the cost of maintaining the common areas along with the costs of insurance, property taxes, office staff, and the like. These fees can be hefty but, as is so often the case, you usually get what you pay for: if the complex is well-run and well-maintained, the fees might be justified. On the other hand, if the complex does not have a good maintenance program and a reserve fund for major repairs, you might well find yourself digging deep in your pocket to pay for expensive problems. **NOTE:** Condo fees **do not** cover the cost of property management services for vacation rental condos. These fees are over and above the monthly condo association fees.

Insurance.   Insurance for a condominium differs from that for a single-family home. The condominium association insures the building, while owners of individual condos insure the contents of their condos. Be sure to ask your condo association whether things like wallpaper, carpeting, and the expensive ceramic tile you plan to install are considered contents or part of the building.

WHAT TO LOOK FOR IN A VACATION CONDO

Before you decide to make a purchase offer on a vacation condo at the beach, you will want to know the following.

> o Are employees of the management firm located in an office on site? Chances are that the property will be better maintained and that problems will be resolved more quickly if employees are on site every day.

o What is the overall condition and appearance of the property? Are the grounds well-maintained? Are walkways, driveways, and parking areas in good repair? If the grass is knee-high and railings are hanging askew, you can bet that there are major repairs needed in areas that are less visible.

o Does the condo association have a reserve account set aside to cover future repairs? If not, you may find that owners are suddenly hit with big bills when it's time for big repairs.

o Does the association or management company have contracts with professional companies to maintain the more complicated amenities such as swimming pools and elevators?

o How is the building constructed? Good construction will keep future assessment for repairs to a minimum. With a condo, as with a single-family home, the services of a professional inspector can be a very good investment in protecting your financial interests.

o What is the history of assessments (additional fees) over the last five to ten years?

In summary, like everything else in this life, there are both pros and cons to condo ownership. On the plus side, a condominium offers you ownership of a vacation property at the beach — a place you can decorate to your own taste and to which you can return, year after year. It's a plus, too, that you won't be burdened with exterior maintenance. And, if you are a woman who plans to spend time at the beach alone, you may feel an extra measure of safety knowing that you have neighbors in such close proximity. Finally, condo ownership can provide you with amenities such as pools, tennis courts, and exercise rooms that you might not be able to afford on your own.

The down side? Condos do not appreciate as much as single-family homes. Then, too, the very proximity to neighbors that is a plus to some is a definite drawback to others who need more "psychological space." There are also many rules and regulations by which condo owners must abide, so you do give up some of your freedom of choice when you buy into the condo lifestyle.

OBTAINING A MORTGAGE

Few of us are fortunate enough to be able to pay cash when purchasing a second home. That means that we must finance our homes through that great American institution — the mortgage. Since you have many options to choose from in terms of lenders, terms, and rates, it's to your benefit to shop very carefully for your mortgage.

MORTGAGE SOURCES

There are three primary sources through which you can obtain a mortgage: a mortgage banker, a mortgage broker, and an independent bank. Let's consider each, in turn.

> o **Mortgage Banker.** A mortgage bank is a bank whose primary source of income is through making, and subsequently selling, mortgages. The entire loan process is handled "in house" so if you apply to such a bank for your mortgage, the loan officer will

be able to tell you exactly what documentation you must provide and what requirements you must meet in order for your loan to be approved.

This is certainly convenient, one-stop shopping. But be aware that your mortgage will not remain at this bank. Instead, it will be sold on the secondary market (e.g. Freddie Mac, Fannie Mae). For the most part, if your mortgage is sold on the secondary market, you won't be inconvenienced in any way. Still, there is a certain comfort factor in knowing that your mortgage is held by your local bank and that your banker is someone you know and with whom you do business on a regular basis.

o **Mortgage Broker.** A mortgage broker is an independent company or individual, usually identified in advertisements as a "mortgage company." The broker/agency accepts your application for a mortgage and then shops around to find a mortgage banker who will finance your loan.

Unfortunately, each bank and every underwriter has specific requirements about information necessary to process a loan application. This means that, if you apply for a mortgage with a mortgage broker, you are likely to find yourself awash in a sea of seemingly endless requests for information — much of which will strike you as inane. The entire process, as one of us discovered the hard way, can be seriously crazy-making.

o **Independent Bank.** Most independent banks prefer to make large agricultural, business, auto, and residential loans. Many, however, will agree to mortgage vacation homes as a good-will gesture to keep your other business dealings with their bank.The loan officer at an independent bank will tell you exactly what information and documentation is necessary to process your loan application.

We prefer to do business with these independent banks for the comfort factor noted above. However, you should know that, in years to come, an independent bank may be bought out by a larger bank and, in the end, your mortgage may be held by a bank with which you are not familiar.

TYPES OF MORTGAGES

For which type of mortgage should you apply — a fixed-rate, variable-rate, or a balloon mortgage?

o **Fixed Rate Mortgage.** Under most circumstances, the best mortgage is a fixed-rate mortgage. If your bank is reluctant to give you a fixed-rate mortgage on a beach house, think about what other assets you might use for collateral to secure this type of loan.

If — like most vacation-home buyers — you are a middle-aged person who owns a home outright or you have built up substantial equity in your principal residence, you have an edge. Since most people in this position would give up eating before defaulting on a mortgage payment, lending institutions consider them a very good credit risk. Knowing this, you might consider mortgaging your personal residence rather than your beach house in order to secure the best loan terms.

o **Adjustable Rate Mortgage.** Adjustable rate mortgages can move not more than 2 percent at any adjustment, nor can they move more than 6 percent over the life of the loan. Thus, a starting rate of 7 1/4 could increase to 9 1/4 after a year and even to 13 1/4 after three years. Adjustments are based on a set formula of the Treasury Bill Index or some other nationally based index. For a comparison of monthly payments per $100,000 borrowed on fixed-rate and variable-rate mortgages, see Table 1 below.

o **Balloon Mortgage.** Balloon mortgages are inherently dangerous unless you have substantial liquid assets. If, for example, you held a balloon mortgage when Jimmy Carter was president, you saw your rate increase from 8 percent to 16 percent. While we hope that the Federal Reserve Board will prevent a similar scenario in the future, there are no guarantees. Thus, we think you would be well advised to avoid a balloon mortgage.

Table 1

ADJUSTABLE V. FIXED RATE MORTGAGES					
MONTHLY COST PER $100,000 BORROWED					
ADJUSTABLE RATE				FIXED RATE	
POTENTIAL INCREASE					
FROM:		TO:			
%	PMT.	%	PMT.	%	PMT.
4.75	$522	10.75	$933	6.875	$657
6.5	$632	12.5	$1067	7.0	$665
7.25	$682	13.25	$1126	7.25	$682

MORTGAGE CONSIDERATIONS

Just as in the case of your principal residence, there are other issues to be considered when you finance your beach house. Among them are the following:

> o **Points Versus Rates.** Points are a fee charged by the mortgage holder for granting a loan. A point is 1 percent of the amount of the loan. For example, if you are charged 5 points on a loan of $100,000, the cost would be $5,000.

Some people would consider a higher interest rate preferable to paying points. However, if you plan to keep the house for more than seven years, you might benefit from paying points, as the example below indicates.

EXAMPLE: 30-year fixed rate mortgage of $100,000.

6.875% and 5 points   **VS**   **8% and 0 pts.**

$656.93/mo. and $5,000 points   **$733.77/mo.**
Difference in payments = $76.84
Points ($5,000) divided by Difference ($76.84) = 66 months:
thus,
points would have been paid off by lower monthly payments
in 5 years, 6 months.

Now, let's look at the costs for the life of the loan.
 8%   **$733.77 X 360 (30 years) = $264,157.20**
 6.875%   **$656.93 X 360 (30 years) = $236,494.80**
                    $27,662.40
                    - $5,000.00 points paid
                    = $22,662.40 saved over life
                       of loan

---

o **Prepaying the Mortgage.** As you probably know, in the early years of a mortgage, most of the money you pay each month goes toward paying the interest on the loan. In the later years of the loan, most of your monthly payment goes toward paying off the principal. Since few lending institutions penalize you for making extra payments against the principal, you can save thousands of dollars over the life of your loan by making extra payments against the principal as early in the loan as possible. You can do this monthly, annually, or whenever you choose.

o **Thirty-year versus Fifteen-year Mortgage.** Before you even begin to shop for a mortgage, you should have an idea of the goals you hope to achieve by buying a vacation home at the beach. Do you plan to use the house as a rental property for a period of time and then move into the house when you retire? If so, a 30-year fixed mortgage might be best for you. In fact, if that is the case, you might want to pre-pay the mortgage during the summer months when the rent money is rolling in and then drop back to your required payments in the winter months when there is little or no rental income.

On the other hand, you may plan to use the house strictly as an investment. In that case, you will want to pay for it as quickly as possible, sell it, and use the profit for other investments. Under these circumstances, a higher monthly debt might be worthwhile.

INSURANCE

You may be surprised — as we were — to learn that homeowner's insurance is available only for houses in which you actually reside and for vacation homes that are rented for fewer than 14 days. As the owner of a rental beach home, you are eligible only for certain types of insurance and your coverage will not be at all comparable to that provided under your current homeowner's policy.

The insurance industry is regulated by each state, so there will be differences across states. However, you should expect to find the following types of insurance available to you.

FIRE AND CASUALTY ("HAZARD") INSURANCE

This type of insurance most closely approximates traditional homeowner's insurance. If your beach house is destroyed by fire, the structure can be insured for replacement value but the contents of the house will be covered only at depreciated value, unless you are willing to pay an exorbitant price for coverage. And the "casualty" portion of the policy has some important exclusions. If, for example, your septic system backs up and floods rooms at ground level, the damage will probably not be covered by insurance.

On the other hand, this type of insurance does cover damage due to wind. (In fact, people who reside at the beach and therefore carry homeowner's insurance often carry this specific wind-damage coverage, as well.) Some states have formed insurance pools to cover wind damage, due to the exceptionally high risk of such damage in certain areas. What is covered under the term "wind damage" is limited to damage directly caused by wind. Thus, if the wind blows shingles off your roof and the roof leaks, causing damage to the interior of the house, insurance will reimburse you for the damage. If, however, wind-driven rain enters the interior of the house through an electrical conduit whose seal disintegrated under harsh weather conditions, you are not covered for the damage you incur as a result. In both cases, wind-driven rain caused interior damage, but wind is considered the primary culprit only in the first instance.

After Hurricane Andrew devastated the southern Florida coast in 1992, the building code in Dade County, Florida, was revised to require that all exterior openings — that is, windows and doors — be protected with shutters or impact-resistant glass.[*] Shutters, which protect your windows from flying debris in a severe storm, are available in a variety of styles, including those which roll down from an overhead metal box (rolling shutters); those which slide horizontally across the window (accordion shutters); those which drop into place from above the window (Bahama shutters); and those which rest flush against the house and can be closed over the windows when a severe storm threatens (colonial shutters).

RESIDENTIAL CRIME INSURANCE

This insurance provides coverage for robbery and theft by an intruder — that is, someone who is **not** a tenant. If a tenant steals from you, you may recoup your loss by means of the security deposit or through legal means, such as small claims court, but you will not be covered by insurance for such losses.

Residential crime insurance policies are issued only if you have what the insurance company determines to be sufficient locks on all windows and exterior doors (e.g. dead bolt locks on hinged doors, bars on sliding doors) and the policy is in effect only if there is evidence of forced entry. As is the case with fire and casualty insurance, however, the stolen goods are covered only to their depreciated value, not their replacement value.

---

[*] Sullivan, A.C. "Storm Watch." **Coastal Living**, 1997, 1(3) p. 148-151.

FLOOD INSURANCE

Flood damage is covered in much the same way as wind damage: that is, the proximate cause of the damage must be from high rising water and contents are insured only for depreciated value. While the law does not require you to have flood insurance, you will not be able to obtain a mortgage in a flood-prone area without it.

Just as states underwrite wind-damage insurance in high risk areas, the federal government underwrites flood insurance under the National Flood Insurance Program (NFIP), established by Congress to make flood insurance available at affordable rates to those who live in flood hazard areas. It is administered through the Federal Insurance Administration under the Federal Emergency Management Agency. Individual policies are handled by local insurance agents but coverage is available only to those who live in communities that agree to implement regulations such as zoning laws and building codes that reduce the likelihood of future flood damage in their areas. In such communities, new construction is stringently regulated in terms of construction standards and "setback" restrictions; that is, the distance between an ocean-front structure and the ocean itself.

Federal flood insurance, which is available only to a maximum of $250,000 on the structure, covers damage to the structure itself caused by flooding, including damage from waves. Both contents and structure are insured for depreciated value. Flood insurance does not cover damage from other events such as the high winds that accompany hurricanes, nor does it cover damage to land resulting from floods, waves, or erosion.

In fact, it is not possible to obtain insurance that covers erosion. This is not surprising, since ocean-front property is subject to long-term erosion, called "beach migration," associated with rising sea levels. Erosion can also occur as the result of severe storms but, since the beach usually replenishes itself afterwards, this is considered short-term erosion. Be aware, however, that such erosion — short-term or not — means that dune decks, walkways and steps to the beach may need to be replaced at intervals, depending on the whims of Mother Nature.

If you are building an ocean-front or sound-front home, you can reduce the risk of damage from floods and erosion by building as far toward the landward end of your lot as possible. You can also lower your flood insurance premiums by using construction techniques designed to help withstand flooding, such as raising the house on pilings higher than those generally required and sinking pilings more than five feet below the surface.

LIABILITY INSURANCE

Whether or not you use your beach house as a rental property — but most especially if you do — you need liability insurance. In fact, some property management firms will not take you on as a client without liability insurance. One of the best ways in which to obtain such coverage is to take out an <u>umbrella policy</u> in conjunction with the homeowner's policy on your principal residence. Umbrella policies can provide liability coverage in the amount of a million dollars and up on all of your properties, vehicles, and so on. They are relatively inexpensive and, we think, invaluable.

CHAPTER FOUR

FURNISHING AND OUTFITTING
YOUR BEACH HOUSE

Furnishing and decorating a beach house is a task that is very different from the way in which most of us go about furnishing and decorating our principal residences. In our own homes, furnishings and decorations are collected one piece at a time, over the years. For example, if you take a look in your kitchen you'll probably find some knives, pots, bowls, and serving utensils handed down from parents, grandparents, and various room-mates, friends, and long-departed lovers. Decorative objects, too, have been gathered one at a time — the picture that's perfect over the buffet, the console table that fits so well in the entry area, the candlesticks you found on a trip to Maine that look so great on the mantle.

In contrast, when you furnish a beach home or other vacation rental property, it's a wham-bam-thank-you-m'am operation. Everything goes into place at once, from silverware and china for twelve or twenty-four, to the pieces of art and the charming little knick-knacks that provide the finishing touches.

ONE-STOP SHOPPING

When it comes to furnishing and outfitting a beach house, you have a choice: you can elect to put all, or most, of the house together by yourself or you can take the one-stop shopping approach. Many furniture stores at the beach are designed to provide "whole house" orders and offer discounts on such purchases. The salespeople are usually knowledgable and able to provide invaluable advice about furniture arrangements, fabrics, and finishes that will serve well in a rental home at the beach.

Unlike furniture stores in other locations, furniture stores at the beach often offer a wide selection of kitchen equipment and linens for the bedroom and bathroom. Many also offer a delivery package; that is, for a nominal fee, they will clean your cabinets, deliver the kitchen equipment you've purchased, remove price tags, wash all of the equipment, and put it away. They will also deliver bed linens and make the beds. At the time of this writing, the fee in the Outer Banks area from stores such as Daniels in Kitty Hawk, North Carolina, averages between $100 and $150 to provide this service.

Depending on the size of the house, this fee might be the best money you ever spent. Imagine the work involved in loading, carrying, and unpacking 30 cups, saucers, plates, and cereal dishes, not to mention all of the accompanying glassware, silverware, and serving pieces. Then imagine the time it takes to remove price tags (a devilish task in itself) and to wash all of these items and put them away. Whew! It's easy to see that utilizing the store service will save an enormous amount of wear and tear on you.

THE DO-IT-YOURSELF APPROACH

If you have the time and the energy, you may be able to save money by eschewing one-stop shopping in favor of furnishing the house yourself. This is especially true if you live near a discount outlet such as Greenfront, a well-known furniture and accessories store in Farmville, Virginia.

Be sure, too, to check out the merchandise at the discount stores at the beach, including stores like Wal-Mart. In beach locations, these stores carry merchandise tailored to the beach environment and are a good place to purchase high chairs, port-a-cribs, and other utilitarian items people expect to find in a beach house.

If you love to shop and you really enjoy the thrill of tracking down a bargain, the do-it-yourself approach is likely to appeal to you. Be prepared, however, to spend a lot of time and effort, since you may have to visit many stores in order to put it all together. You will also have to coordinate delivery from these same stores.

Whether you choose one-stop shopping, the do-it-yourself approach, or some combination of the two, remember that you may have to wait three to six months for the furniture you order to arrive. Remember, too, to take a copy of your house plans with you when you set out on your shopping trips. (The distance from "this" wall to "that" wall is important when you're buying a sofa.) If you have a color scheme in mind, take along some fabric swatches or some paint samples: without a visual example, your idea of "sunny yellow" might translate to the salesperson as "screaming saffron."

If possible, arrange your schedule so that you can spend a few hours a day across several days making your selections. In an emergency, you **can** furnish an entire seven-bedroom house in a day. Of course, you will then be so dazed and exhausted that, come the next day, you won't have the foggiest idea what color sofas you ordered for the great room — but at least the worst will be behind you.

THE BASICS

Whether you use the services of a decorator, do one-stop shopping at a beach furniture store, or decide to assemble the furnishings yourself, there are well-established guidelines for furnishing and equipping rental homes at the beach. Let's go through these guidelines, room by room.

THE KITCHEN

Although people who vacation at the beach are usually rather casual about meals, you can bet that in every group there is at least one person who wants to take advantage of the fresh seafood, vegetables, and other goodies available at the shore to show off his or her culinary skills. This is the person to whom your kitchen equipment speaks volumes and woe unto you if that person is disappointed by your kitchen.

Of course, all appliances should be in good working order. If you're building or buying a house that is under construction, you have an opportunity to select the major appliances yourself. We suggest that you select from the mid-range: top-of-the-line appliances have more bells and whistles than your guests are likely to need and only increase the chance of something breaking down, while low-end appliances won't hold up under heavy use. We also suggest that you consider installing two dishwashers and two refrigerators, particularly in homes that accommodate more than fifteen guests. It's a little more costly in terms of initial outlay, but your guests will appreciate your thoughtfulness for years to come.

Cookware, too, should be in good condition, which means that you should either purchase top-quality pots and pans or plan to replace such things as frying pans quite often. A list of essential cookware is provided in Appendix A, along with a list of everything else needed for a well-equipped kitchen.

Experienced rental agencies suggest that you provide a minimum of one-and-one-half place settings of china and silverware for each occupant (thus, if your house accommodates ten people, they sugggest that you buy for fifteen). We would encourage you to provide **two** place settings per person. We also recommend that you purchase extra pieces to replace lost and broken items so that everything will match over the years.

Provide an array of drinking glasses — juice glasses, large and small tumblers, beer mugs, and wine glasses. Be sure to provide enough glasses for at least twice the number of guests your home accommodates: people tend to drink a lot at the beach. Have a large assortment of plastic glassware on hand for little people, too, to minimize breakage and injuries.

And, speaking of plastic: it's a good idea to provide a generous assortment of inexpensive, light-weight plastic containers with tight-fitting lids so guests can take home any leftovers at the end of their stay. (This helps insure that your sturdier covered containers don't disappear.)   Check take-out food stores near your principal residence to find one willing to sell you a couple of dozen containers and lids at cost or a bit above.

If you, yourself, are an enthusiastic cook, you know that you would be hard pressed to do without a food processor, a pasta machine, an espresso machine, and other sundry items. Go ahead and leave this equipment for your guests to use: guests who are not familiar with their use will leave them alone, while those who do use them will already know how to use and care for them.

If you keep copies of your favorite cookbooks at your beach house, go ahead and leave them out for your guests to enjoy, too. Sure, they'll sustain some wear and tear — but isn't that what they're there for? The more that you convey the attitude of "my home is your home," the greater the likelihood that your guests will respond by caring for your house as if it really **were** their own.

THE GREAT ROOM

Since this is the room in which people will congregate, it should be particularly comfortable and inviting. Give some thought in advance as to how people like to spend their time together in groups. Because there will always be at least one or two bodies parked in front of the television/VCR, place your sturdiest and most comfortable couches and chairs where these people can have the best view and place end tables close at hand to hold drinks and munchies. If you're buying new couches and chairs, be mindful of the wear and tear they will sustain and order arm covers for all upholstered pieces. Try, too, to select pieces that lend themselves to being slip-covered when the original fabric becomes shabby and stained.

A good sound system (radio/CD player/tape deck) is a must. Don't worry about children damaging the equipment: most children today are more knowledgable about high-tech equipment than many adults. If you leave CDs and tapes for your guests to enjoy, be judicious in your selections.

Few people will walk off with your collection of classical music but tapes and CDs that appeal to teenagers might not be there upon your return. (This is true of video tapes, as well, as we have both learned to our dismay.)

Many families who vacation at the beach have a tradition of playing board games or doing jig-saw puzzles in the evening. Be sure that their needs will be met by providing a game table with good overhead lighting.

With all of the hub-bub and commotion that usually takes place there, only a few stalwart souls will actually attempt to read in the great room. For those who do, however, provide good lighting.

THE BEDROOMS

On the theory that guests won't be spending much time in their bedrooms, many misguided beach-house owners skimp on the details that make a bedroom comfortable. Children, worn out from hours of playing in the sand and the sun, don't really notice or care about their sleeping space, but it's not safe to assume that the same is true of adult guests. In fact, after a day spent in the company of others, many adults long to retreat to the quiet sanctuary of a comfortable bedroom for some "down time." What makes a bedroom feel like home?

The Bed and the Bedding. Although it should be obvious that a comfortable mattress heads the list, you would be surprised at how many people try to cut corners on such essential items. Our advice: select a good quality mattress and box spring for every bed in your home.[*] When it comes time to replace a worn-out mattress set, don't try to skimp by putting a new mattress on an old box spring: mattress and box spring work as a unit and putting a new mattress on an old box spring could void your warranty.

---

[*] The March, 1997, issue of *Consumer Reports* has an informative article on purchasing and caring for mattresses. To obtain a copy via mail or fax, call 1-800-766-9988 and request Report Number 9554. The charge is $7.75

At the time of this writing, you can expect to spend the following: about $450 for a twin set, $600 for a double, $800 for a queen, and $1,000 for a king. Remember that king- and queen-size beds are most popular in bedrooms for adult guests.

To extend the life of your mattresses and box springs, be sure to rotate them, side to side and head to toe, at the start or the end of every rental season during the first four years, since this is the time they will wear most rapidly.

Pillows, too, are very important. In fact, almost nothing else spells "tacky" quite as much as thin, lumpy bed pillows. Buy good quality, hypoallergenic pillows and replace them as soon as they begin to show wear. We recommend supplying two pillows per person for all beds which might be occupied by adults.

If you invest in good mattresses and good pillows, as we think you should, protect your investment by covering the mattresses with mattress covers and the pillows with zippered pillow covers. In rooms that are likely to be used by children, mattresses should be covered by a water-proof mattress protector beneath the mattress cover.

You must also provide at least one blanket per bed in a rental home. Again, we think that more is better and would urge you to keep a few extra blankets on hand. We have found that the best buy in terms of longevity are nylon blankets with a velour finish such as Vellux (TM). They don't pill or fray and they withstand repeated washings well.

What about bedspreads? Should you invest in expensive custom-made spreads or opt for less costly comforters that are so widely available? While common sense might seem to dictate the latter, we're not so sure that it's the most economical approach in the long run, at least for bedrooms which are likely to be occupied by adults. Although department store comforters are inexpensive and available in a wide range of colors, they don't hold up well after a couple of washings. In fact, after a couple of years of replacing such comforters at regular intervals in our principal residences, both of us opted for much more expensive custom-made spreads. We've been amazed at how well these spreads have held up, cleaning after cleaning, under the onslaughts of dogs, cats, kids, and husbands. We think that the same is true in beach houses, as well. You might have to have the spreads relined every few years since odd and inexplicable stains tend to appear on the linings, but the cost is nominal compared to the cost of replacing comforters every season or two and the look is so much nicer.

Whether you opt for department-store or custom-made, however, select a busy pattern over a plain fabric. Busy patterns are much better at hiding the inevitable stray stain or mishap.

   Other Amenities. When your guests retire to their rooms, some look forward to watching their favorite late-night television program or curling up in bed with a good book. Thus, in addition to providing a television in bedrooms likely to be used by adults, be sure that your guests have good bed-side lighting on **both** sides of the bed. And don't skimp on light-bulbs: high-wattage three-way bulbs are expensive but the cost is more than offset by the comfort factor. Remember, if your beach house commands up-scale rents, your guests are entitled to up-scale accommodations. Be thoughtful and leave replacement bulbs in a handy location. Give some thought, too, to how your guests will use their rooms during waking hours. Obviously, they will be dressing and undressing in their rooms, so they will need ample drawer and closet space to stow their belongings. Closets should have as many hooks as you can squeeze in: be sure to use the sturdiest ones you can find, since flimsy plastic hooks won't last through the first season. And, it's an odd fact of life that those wire hangers that seem to reproduce themselves in alarming numbers in your principal residence will perversely vanish with equal speed from your beach house. We have no explanation for this eerie phenomenon, but be prepared to restock every closet with hangers at the start of the rental season each year. (We would warn against metal hangers due to rust problems, but ours have never lasted long enough for this to actually be a problem.)

It's also thoughtful to put at least one chair in every adult bedroom. If you have room for a comfortable chair, so much the better: those who want to duck into their rooms for some quiet time with a book or in front of the television will appreciate a cozy chair — and it will save your bedspread from excessive wear and tear.

Finally, don't forget to include a large mirror in every bedroom that will be used by adults. It's annoying and frustrating to have to dress without checking the results in a mirror, even if you're only putting on a bathing suit.

THE BATHROOMS

Nothing spells luxury like a well-lighted, well-appointed bathroom. And nothing spells "cheap" more than a dank, dark cubby-hole in which people must go through contortions in order to wash, shave, and apply make-up. Be sure, therefore, that you provide good lighting and lots of storage space in your bathrooms. While a vanity under the sink can provide storage for larger items, you should also include medicine cabinets in which guests can stash make-up, shaving equipment, and pill bottles. Since metal rusts so quickly in a beach environment, buy plastic or wooden medicine chests rather than metal. You might have to shop around a bit, but it's worth it.

You should also avoid glass shower doors. Neither your guests nor your cleaning crew will have the patience to wipe them clean of soap scum and they will soon develop an ugly, clouded, opaque appearance. Instead, use shower curtains. We have found that fabric curtains, in combination with plastic liners, work very well. If you buy sturdy liners, you can put them through the washing machine at the end of the season to remove mildew and restore a fresh appearance. If you buy liners of lesser quality, throw them away and replace them every season.

Bathrooms at the beach should also have plenty of towel rods (ceramic rods are best in terms of longevity). There should also be an abundance of sturdy ceramic hooks so that guests can hang their towels and bathing suits to dry.

If you really want to make your female guests happy — and, remember, they are the ones who usually determine where the family will vacation — include a counter-top or wall-mounted make-up mirror with 3X magnification.

Soap dishes should be provided in all bathrooms. You might also want to provide toothbrush holders and bathroom tumblers. Of course, a small wastebasket is a must in every bathroom.

THE FINISHING TOUCHES

PICTURES AND PRINTS

Naturally, many of the prints and paintings you hang in your beach house will reflect a beach theme. Give some thought to your selections, however, and be sure to vary them a bit to avoid monotony: you might, for example, include some wildlife prints or some floral scenes. For a light and airy look, use one big picture in place of many small ones, particularly in rooms with cathedral ceilings. Be sure that all wall-hung art is firmly anchored in place so that each piece remains straight, in spite of frontal assaults by guests and cleaning crews.

DECORATIVE OBJECTS

Again, it's fine to have a beach theme, but don't go overboard. Remember that every other house on the beach has lamps shaped like shells, along with coasters shaped like star-fish. Make your house stand out by including some pieces that blend with the decor but reflect a different theme. At our own beach houses, for example, one of us has mixed in some oriental pieces, while the other has blended Caribbean art and sculpture into the overall design.

As is the case with wall-hung art, one or two large pieces look better in a big room than a lot of little miniature pieces. If you want to include an expensive or fragile item in the decor, just be sure to put it where little hands can't mangle or break it.

It's a nice touch, too, to include some decorative objects to which your guests can contribute their own offerings. A big basket partially filled with shells invites contributions from your guests, for example, and makes them feel more like the place is truly theirs.

For the very reason that you want your guests to consider the place as theirs, you should avoid placing personal objects such as family photos in the house. It's fine to hang beach photos you've taken of glorious sunsets or animals romping on the beach: it's not a good idea to bedeck the place with framed pictures of your children or your mother-in-law.

EXTERIOR EQUIPMENT

Since your guests will want to spend as much time as possible out of doors, you should ensure that they can do so in comfort. This means that you must provide ample deck furniture to accommodate your guests. If your beach house is in an area subject to high winds — as so many beaches are — choose your deck furniture accordingly. Light-weight plastic furniture is popular and inexpensive but, in high winds, such furniture can quickly become misguided missles. One of us watched in horror as our plastic table for six sailed off the upper deck like a tossed frisbee and ended up in a thousand pieces in our neighbor's yard.

Our recommendation: on unprotected decks, use either heavy wooden furniture or opt for the new recycled poly-wood outdoor furniture. Poly-wood comes in your choice of three colors, never needs painting, and is heavy enough to resist all but hurricane-force winds. The cost of a wooden Adirondak chair is approximately $100, while a poly-wood chair costs around $150. These prices are significantly higher than those you would pay for plastic furniture, but worth it in the long run.

Provide an outdoor shower (two, for larger homes) and a fish-cleaning station with a water supply. Both will please your guests, while reducing wear and tear on the house itself.

Garden hoses should be available on every level, from the ground up. This allows your guests to hose off everything from spray-covered vehicles and house windows to sandy feet and soggy pets. We also leave a sturdy plastic tub outside each of the main doors to encourage even the youngest beach-goers to rinse sand from their feet before entering.

Of course, your guests will expect an outdoor grill on which to cook steaks, fish, and in-season vegetables. Since fire regulations at the beach usually prohibit grilling on decks, don't even think about providing any kind of portable grill or hibachi (and dispose of any that your guests leave behind when they depart). Instead, have a charcoal grill sunk into a cement base in a location that offers your house some protection in case of high winds. Although neither you nor I would consider cooking out under such circumstances, it's surprising what some people will do.

For storing beach equipment, consider having large wooden storage chests installed on your deck or your dune deck. These bins can hold beach toys, umbrellas, rafts, life preservers, coolers, and the like. You might be pleasantly surprised to find that guests often add to the collection. Do be sure, however, that the more expensive items are marked with your address and that storage chests can be solidly secured against the high winds that often batter a beach environment.

Large, sturdy trash receptacles should be provided in sufficient numbers to ensure that your guests can dispose of all trash properly. Stencil your name (or the name of your cottage) and the street address on the cans.

CHAPTER FIVE

MARKETING AND RENTING YOUR BEACH HOUSE

MAXIMIZING YOUR RENTAL INCOME

Whether your beach house is ocean front or several blocks away from the ocean, there are numerous things you can do to both maximize your rates and ensure that your house will be rented throughout the season.

As a rule of thumb, **the closer the house is to the beach, the higher the rent.** Of course, the properties closest to the beach are also the most expensive in terms of purchase price. That leads us to the next rule of thumb: **the amount of rent you can expect to charge is directly proportional to the number of people the house can accommodate** — the more people, the higher the rent. Thus, maximizing the number of people the house can accommodate makes good business sense. It's difficult to justify spending close to $300,000 for an ocean-front lot (that's right — just the lot) and building a house that accommodates only six or eight people.

Consider the following ways to increase sleeping capacity in your beach house:

o If you build, build the maximum number of bedrooms and bathrooms permitted by the building code.

o If you buy, check to see if you can add additional bedrooms.

o Add sleep sofas in large bedrooms and in living areas.

o Use pyramid bunk beds (the bottom bunk is a double bed) or a pyramid/trundle bed combination. A bedroom containing a pyramid bunk bed and a pyramid/trundle combination, for example, could sleep seven people. (**You** might not want to be one of the seven, but kids don't seem to mind a bit.)

o Provide roll-away beds and futons for kids.

MAKING YOUR HOUSE STAND OUT
FROM THE OTHERS

Although some beach-goers prefer simple and inexpensive cottages, many of today's vacationers are more luxury-oriented. When they spend big bucks to rent a house at the beach, they expect amenities they don't have at home. Hot tubs, saunas, jacuzzis, and swimming pools attract renters, so look for properties that have these amenities or have the potential for them to be added. An existing house might not have space for a sauna or a pool but hot tubs fit nicely onto almost any size porch or deck, provided that appropriate support is added. Swimming pools that are heated in the spring and fall can increase your rental rate considerably in these seasons.

Other amenities that attract renters include:

o King- and queen-size beds

o Pool tables, ping pong tables

o Exercise equipment

o Basketball hoops

o Bicycles

o High chairs, port-a-cribs, playpens

o Barbecue grills

o Video library or free passes to a nearby video store

o Under-counter ice maker

o Gas fireplace

o Televisions, stereos, VCRs

o Linen service

You might also want to consider permitting pets in your beach house. Although it is generally acknowledged that pets cause less damage than children in rental cottages, the number of rental homes in which pets are permitted is quite limited, so "pet cottages" are in demand and generally command a higher rental. Renters who bring pets to the beach are accustomed to paying a higher security deposit and a flea-spray charge. They are also accustomed to paying a bit more in rent for the privilege of having Fluffy or Muffy accompany them on vacation.

TAKING CARE OF YOUR GUESTS

You've bought or built your beach house. You've furnished and decorated it down to the last detail. Now, how do you go about ensuring that you will have a paying clientele who will return to your house year after year? This is an important point, because "repeat renters" come to feel that they have an interest in the house and generally tend to take good care of it, often leaving behind small items they've purchased, such as books and unusual kitchen tools.

WELCOMING YOUR GUESTS

What do your guests expect when they walk into your beach house? This is a no-brainer: what do **you** expect when you walk into a beach house? Hot and tired from a long trip, you want to walk into a house that is attractively furnished, cool, and sparkling clean.

It's a nice welcoming touch, too, on your arrival to find a package of starter supplies such as a roll of toilet paper, paper towels, a small bottle of dish detergent, and other small but important amenities. You can usually make arrangements with your rental agency to provide such a "welcome basket" at a nominal cost.

A popular trend, particularly in the more expensive beach houses and in the large resort condominiums, is to provide guests with full linen service so they won't have to bring their own bed linens or make up the beds on arrival. Check with your property management firm about the cost and availability of this service.

KEEPING THEM HAPPY

Try to anticipate the needs of your guests. Think about the cottages in which you've stayed in the past: remember how annoying it was to need an item that wasn't there? Maybe it was something small, like a cork screw or a screw driver or a nut cracker for opening crab legs. While no one can think of everything, it's a sure bet that people will have sour memories of your cottage if they reach for too many things that aren't there.

Our "keeping them happy" list includes all of the items that we've listed in Appendices A and B. In addition, we suggest that you personalize your home by adding a guest book in which your guests can record their happy memories of time spent in your house. You might also want to include an array of books, games, and jig-saw puzzles for your guests to enjoy on rainy days. If you provide such amenities, make sure that they are all in good condition at the start of each rental season. When puzzles and games show signs of wear, throw them out and replace them.

If surf fishing or crabbing are popular at your beach, consider supplying fishing and crabbing gear. Equipment for surf-fishing is surprisingly inexpensive and quite sturdy.

For an annual fee paid by the cottage owner, some video stores at the beach offer your guests access to unlimited free videos during their stay in your house. If this is not available in your area, a personal library of video tapes is a good idea. Be forewarned, however: video tapes that appeal to teenagers are likely to disappear, so plan to replace such tapes regularly.

The Big Blue Book. You can help to ensure that your guests will be comfortable in your home — and that your home will survive your guests — by providing them with vital information that will make their vacation easier, safer, and more enjoyable. For this, we suggest that you provide your guests with what we call "The Big Blue Book."

The Big Blue Book is a large loose-leaf binder (which happens to be blue) that is updated every year. It includes the following:

o <u>A letter of welcome to your guests.</u> This letter should describe any peculiarities of the home (e.g. septic system rather than sewer) that might require special care. A sample letter is given below.

o <u>The manufacturer's operating instructions for all equipment and appliances.</u> This will also ensure that you have all your war-ranty information in one place.

o <u>Emergency information</u> for use in both medical emergencies (telephone numbers and locations of medical facilities) and in case of natural disasters such as hurricane evacuation.

o <u>General information</u> about recreational activities, places of interest, restaurants and shops in the area. You might want to leave a collection of guide-books, maps, menus from local restaurants, and the like in a separate folder, a large basket, or a kitchen drawer. Guests often add to these collections and write comments on menus and brochures to benefit other guests.

SAMPLE LETTER TO GUESTS

To Our Guests:

Welcome to our beach house! We hope you will love it here as much as we do. For your convenience, this book contains operating instructions for all equipment and appliances in the house. There is also information concerning medical emergencies and evacuation procedures — although we certainly hope that you will not need this information during your stay.

General Information for All Guests

BATHROOMS: The house is served by a septic system, not a sewer, so non-biodegradable objects like tampons, diapers, and cigarettes should **never** be flushed down the toilets. When using the Jacuzzi, the water level must be above the jets before the Jacuzzi is turned on in order to avoid burning out the motor.

SAUNA: Instructions are posted in the sauna. Please be sure that both the temperature and time controls are turned off after use.

DECK LOCKER: Beach chairs, toys, and boogie boards are stored in the covered locker on the deck.

HOSES: Hoses are available on all levels so that you can rinse sand and ocean-spray from windows, vehicles, and pets.

SUPPLIES: Cleaning equipment is located in the utility closet outside the powder room. Light bulbs, vacuum cleaner bags, a first aid kit, and a flashlight are in the kitchen cabinet closest to the dining area. There is a collection of spices and other kitchen staples for your convenience: if you use the last of something, please replace it for the next guests. The food-storage containers on the top shelf of the cabinet closest to the pow- der room are for your convenience if you wish to take food home with you when you leave.

FIRE EXTINGUISHERS: Fire extinguishers are located in the utility room (first floor), master bedroom closet (second floor), and utility/air conditioning closet (third floor).

TRASH COLLECTION: Trash collection is on Monday and Thursday. The night before, put the trash container at the end of the driveway with the handle facing **away from the road**.

DECK FURNITURE: In very high winds, please secure deck furniture, using bungee cords on railing outside of door to kitchen.

STAINS/SPILLS: A stain-removal/pet clean-up kit is in the red bucket under the kitchen counter closest to the living area. Please, **no Kool-Aid or popsicles in the house**: these stains are impossible to remove from furniture and carpets.

In case of a problem or question, please call _____ (property manager) at _____(phone number).

Have a wonderful vacation!

Sincerely,

_____(your name)

We update our welcome letter every year, noting any changes or new acquisitions.

YOUR PROPERTY MANAGER, YOUR BEST FRIEND

The realty agency which provides your property management services should be — as ours have been — active and involved partners in making your beach house a going concern and a good investment. In fact, as the people on the scene, your property management firm can mean the difference between a beach house that's a delight to own and one that is a chronic headache.

It's important, then, that you give some thought to selecting the right firm to manage your beach house. If you've rented from the same firm over the years and have found their rental agents to be friendly and helpful and their houses clean and well-cared-for, it makes good sense to go with that firm for your own beach house. It's a bonus, too, if the firm belongs to the Vacation Rental Managers Association (VRMA), a trade association that provides seminars and conferences designed to increase profession-alism and customer-service skills among managers of rental vacation homes.* Vendors from around the country attend the VRMA annual con-vention to demonstrate the latest in products like computer software to better manage rental properties and telephone "blocking" services that allow your guests to make long-distance calls but not charge them to your phone. Having all these vendors in one place allows VRMA firms to keep up with the latest advances in a business that is extremely competitive.

What can you expect from your property management agency? Top-notch property management firms provide the following:

> o Advertising designed to attract prospective renters.

> o Experienced and friendly rental agents to make reservations and, while your guests are in residence, answer questions and resolve problems quickly and efficiently.

> o A skilled maintenance crew to provide prompt repairs when needed.

> o A conscientious and thorough cleaning crew (if cleaning ser-vices are part of the management package).

> o An inspector who knows your home down to the last detail and who checks carefully for damage and breakage when guests depart.

A good property manager should also be able to give you many tips about how to market your house to maximum advantage. While we've covered many in this book, there may be other attention-getters in your particular locale that we've overlooked. Your property manager is a good source of information about such amenities and can also advise you about the cost-benefit ratio of any improvements or changes you plan to make.

---

* For a free brochure which lists property management firms affiliated with this associa-tion, contact Vacation Rental Managers Association, Post Office Box 1202, Santa Cruz, CA 95061-1202. Voice mail: (800) 871-8762. E-mail: 3495298@mcimail.com. URL: http//www.VRMA.com.

SELECTING A PROPERTY MANAGEMENT FIRM

We recommend that you interview at least three rental management companies. Obtain answers to the following questions before deciding who will manage your property.

o Do they belong to a trade organization such as the Vacation Rental Managers Association that requires adherence to a code of ethics?

o Do they produce a brochure which contains a picture of your house and a description of amenities?

o Will they place your home on the Internet?

o What is the non-family group policy? This is very important in protecting your house: do you really want to rent your beach house to a college fraternity?

o What commission does the firm charge and what does this commission cover? Fees can vary anywhere between 15 and 60 percent of the weekly rent, depending on the locale and the services included in the fee (linens, cleaning, maintenance, and so on). As a matter of convenience, we prefer a single fee that covers all services needed to keep the house running smoothly and the guests happy. This means that you, as an owner, deal with a single agency instead of several independent companies.

o Do they offer travel insurance to guests? Travel insurance, as we discuss below, protects both you and your guests if a vacation must be interrupted due to adverse weather or to an illness or accident suffered by the guest.

o Do they provide free phone block service, where available? This service allows the owner to make long-distance calls by dialing a code number while guests must use a calling card or reverse the charges on long-distance calls.

o Do reservationists visit each house to gain first-hand knowledge of what they are marketing?

o Is there an inspection program? How often are houses inspected for cleanliness and damage?

o How are maintenance problems handled?

o Do they provide year-end summaries and 1099s?

WORKING WITH YOUR PROPERTY MANAGEMENT FIRM

A great way in which to get to know your property management staff is to invite them all to a wine and cheese party or a cocktail buffet. Such a gathering is best held during the off-season and on a weekday, right after working hours. Make it clear that spouses are also welcome; lay in a hearty supply of good cold cuts, salads, finger foods, and beverages; and be prepared to have a good time.

Be prepared, too, to take everyone on a guided tour of your house, so be sure that every room is spiffed up. The tour, of course, lets your rental agents see your house at its best so they can talk knowledgeably about it with prospective renters. And the party is a nice way to say "Thank you" to the very important people who care for your property in your absence.

If you have selected a good property management firm, you will never regret the percentage you pay them: they will be worth every penny. For example, when a tenant's car caught fire in the carport under our house late one night, our property manager heard the fire-call on her scanner. Recognizing the address, she went directly to the house, where she remained for several hours while the fire officials determined that there was no damage to the house. The next day, she sent the company's maintenance supervisor to double check. Only then, when all was under control, did we receive a phone call about the incident. **That's good property management!**

Of course, most of the services our property management firm has provided have been much less dramatic. For example, when a tenant complained that there were too few deck chairs for the number of occupants, a member of the management staff assessed the situation and agreed with the tenant. Instead of bothering us with the problem, the staff member simply purchased sturdy but inexpensive deck chairs, had them delivered, and billed our account. Only when significant cost is involved (e.g. replacing a dishwasher or a VCR) are we called to approve the expenditure.

Then, too, there have been countless times when our property management company has resolved little problems over the phone, at no charge to us. When a tenant calls to report malfunctioning equipment, for example, the property management staff makes every effort to assess the situation before dispatching a technician. They know to ask, for example, "Is the appliance plugged in?" and "Have you checked the circuit breaker?" before sending someone to the house. After all, you would have to pay for the technician's time, even if all he did was flip a circuit breaker.

TRIP CANCELLATION INSURANCE

An important service that your property manager can provide for your guests is **trip cancellation insurance**. In most resort areas, guests must make a deposit of 50 percent of the total rental fee when reserving a house. Since this deposit is nonrefundable unless the house is rented to another tenant for that time period, they stand to lose a sizeable amount of money if they must cancel. Trip cancellation insurance protects your guests' deposits if they must cancel their vacation plans due to illness or death of a member of the traveling party or a member of the immediate family.

This insurance also covers your guests if their trip is interrupted by such unforeseeable events as illness, injury, or severe weather conditions. If there is a hurricane evacuation order, for example, the insurance company will reimburse your guests for unused rental days, beginning with the day the mandatory evacuation is announced. Under one widely-used plan, for example, if guests have four days or less remaining in their stay after the evacuation order has been lifted but choose to go home and not return for the remaining days, the insurance will reimburse them for all unused days — a policy which is far more generous than reimbursements generally available through vacation rental companies.

Trip cancellation/interruption insurance benefits you as an owner, too, because you will not have to refund money to insured guests for days affected by an evacuation order. Of course, if a guest cancels just a week or two before the final payment is due (usually a month in advance of the guest's arrival), you are still out half the rent for that rental period unless the house can be re-rented. However, if full payment has been made to you, the guest will be fully reimbursed if he has purchased trip cancellation insurance, and you retain your full fee.

CHAPTER SIX

MAINTAINING THE DREAM

EXTERIOR MAINTEANCE

Those of us who spend most of the year inland are constantly amazed at the damage wrought by wind and water on man-made structures at the water's edge. A painted surface that might last for six or seven years or more inland becomes pitted and unsightly after only a few years in a beach environment.

Surf, sun, and salt air will take a heavy toll on all exterior surfaces. The closer to the beach you are, the more you can count on the wind and the weather taking a toll on your house. In fact, if your home is ocean-front, you may find yourself faced with replacing not only the steps at the end of your walkway to the beach, but even sections of the walkway itself.

This can be an expensive undertaking, especially on a regular basis. An experienced local carpenter who is used to handling such projects can often give you good advice about how to locate and design your steps and walkway so that they are less susceptible to damage and less costly to replace when damage does occur.

If you own a beach-front home, be sure to take annual pictures of the dune deck, steps, and other amenities that front directly on the beach. If your property is damaged during a storm, these pictures are invaluable for insurance purposes and to permit you to "re-build" in an area that may be protected by federal law.

Exterior Surfaces.   Most experienced painters at the beach will tell you to plan on repainting exterior surfaces every three to five years. While painters often prefer to spray-paint exterior surfaces, insist that the paint be applied by brush, since this works the paint into the surface of the wood so the paint job lasts longer. Between paintings, check all exterior caulking around doors and windows to be sure that it provides protection against the elements.

All exposed wood, whether or not it has been salt-treated, will require a periodic application of a sealant for protection against the elements. These sealants, which should also provide protection against ultraviolet rays from the relentless sun, have a watery consistency and are easy to apply with garden sprayers or rollers. (If you use a sprayer, be sure that the breeze is blowing away from the house and from cars parked nearby.) Exterior wood should be at least six months old before sealant is applied, so that the wood can absorb the sealant properly. If the wood has been in place for a longer period of time and is dark gray, with mildew spots, you will have to pressure wash the surfaces and allow them to dry completely before applying sealant. Plan to repeat this process every two to three years, first testing a small area by applying sealant: if the wood readily absorbs the sealant, it's time for a re-application of the product.

Swimming Pools and Hot Tubs.   Contract privately to have chemicals added twice weekly in season or have your property management firm take over this responsibility. And don't try to skimp: the blazing sun at the beach causes these chemicals to evaporate more quickly than in your pool or hot tub at home.

Septic Tank.   A much less glamorous but much more essential feature of your home is the lowly septic tank, the receptacle for the waste from sinks, toilets, showers, and bath tubs. Those of us who dwell in the city usually give little thought to these waste products. However, when we become home-owners at the beach, and in doing so inherit a septic tank, it behooves us to become experts on the subject.

Of all the horrible things that can befall the owner of a beach house, certainly one of the worst is having your septic tank back up into the house. If, like so many owners of beach property, if you have a septic tank, be sure to have it checked and cleaned at regular intervals: ask your property manager how often this should be done. Be sure, too, to warn your guests not to put items that are not bio-degradable into the system via sinks or toilets. (See sample letter to guests in Chapter 5.)

Outdoor Grills. Outdoor grills and other exterior metal surfaces are subjected to a tremendous beating at the beach. You can prolong the life span of such equipment by treating rusted areas with a rust-proof paint.

Exterior Faucets and Shower Heads. These fixtures corrode quickly at the beach. Check them in the spring and the fall and replace as needed.

Exterior Lighting. Exterior light fixtures should be checked regularly for corrosion. Because good exterior lighting is such an important safety feature, your cleaning crew should check frequently for burnt-out bulbs.

LANDSCAPING

A natural look, also known as "letting it all grow wild," has long been popular at some of the more relaxed beaches. In recent years, however, there has been a marked trend toward a planned and manicured look, particularly in the newer and more expensive beach communities. If many of your neighbors have adopted a more controlled look, you should, too: keeping up with the neighbors is important in a rental resort community.

At a minimum, you should employ someone to keep weeds under control near the house. You can contract privately for this service or you can have your property manager take over this responsibility.

While hard-surface driveways and parking pads are becoming more popular at the beach, many owners still opt to surface these areas with less-costly pea gravel and river rock. If you elect this option, remember that enormous and unsightly weeds can pop up almost overnight, giving the place a down-at-the-heels appearance. Thus, you will have to contract to have weeds kept down in the driveway and parking area during the season. You will also have to have additional gravel delivered at intervals to keep these areas looking presentable.

GARDENING AT THE BEACH

"If I had my choice, it would be a garden by the sea," notes Daniel Foley, author of the classic *Gardening by the Sea*.* "A place where untempered winds and ocean spray challenge the most competent of gardeners...where sunlit dew makes even the tiniest plants appear like jewels in the early morning sun ... where the the mingled fragrances of flowers, mixed with the salt of sea breezes, give the air a bracing freshness."

Depending on the region of the country in which your beach house is located, the environment for gardening ranges from virtually ideal to quite challenging, indeed. Gardeners who live along the coast in the Pacific Northwest, for example, are the envy of gardeners and horticulturists the world over, since this region is famous for its temperate climate. Of course, summer fogs in some areas place limits on sun-loving plants but the mild winters and long growing seasons along this coast make the area a gardener's dream.

Along California's 1,200-mile coast, summer fogs and temperatures moderated by the ocean also create a hospitable environment for a great variety of plants. In fact, in the spring-like climate that prevails year 'round, coastal gardeners must actually take care to avoid some plants that grow too enthusiastically and become invasive pests. Since erosion control is important, gardeners who live on coastal bluffs should avoid plants such as ice plant and large trees such as Monterey pine which can add excessive weight to fragile seaside cliffs and increase erosion.

New England beaches offer wonderful growing conditions for gardeners, in spite of a relatively short growing season. Drive along any road through Cape Cod during the summer, for example, and you will see luxurious and well-tended gardens surrounding even the tiniest of homes and

---

* "The Southeast Coast." In *Taylor's Guide to Seashore Gardening*.

overflowing flower boxes in window after window. Interestingly, hybrid tea roses and rambler roses, so prone to fungus in other areas actually benefit from the fungicidal action of drifing ocean spray so roses bloom in vigorous profusion in coastal gardens here and on Nantucket and Martha's Vineyard. For sound advice on gardening on the Northeast Coast from Canada to Virginia, consult *Seaside Gardening*, written by Theodore James and photographed by Harry Haralambou (Harry N. Abrams, Inc., 1995).

On the other hand, beaches on the barrier islands that stretch along the Southeast Coast of the United States pose special challenges to the seashore gardener. Here, the gardener is limited to plants that can withstand a combination of fierce summer sun, poor soil, and salt-laden winds. Beach sand, for example, is not a good growing medium for most plants because it retains little moisture and has little or no organic material. And, as landscape architect Glenn Morris notes,[*] summer temperatures of dune sand can easily reach 140 degrees F. If you were a plant, he asks, would you choose this place to put down roots?

In such areas, plan to bring in topsoil and mulch by the truckload if you want to grow anything other than native "scrub" vegetation. In such an environment, too, you can forget fussy, heat-sensitive plants that demand constant babying, particularly if you are not there to tend to their needs regularly during the summer months. Instead, look to the variety of wonderful plants that will not only survive but thrive, at the beach. For detailed information, consult *Seacoast Plants of the Carolinas*,[*] an inexpensive but comprehensive source of information about using plants for both conservation and beautification in coastal areas.

Gardeners who live along the Southeast Coast and the Gulf Coast can usually enjoy the pleasures of the garden throughout the year and can indulge in such exotics as palm trees, citrus and banana trees, and all sorts of showy tropical plants. However, sudden drops in temperature pose a hazard to the more sensitive tropical plants that otherwise do well in these

---

[*] Available from UNC Sea Grant, Box 8605, North Carolina State University, Raleigh, NC 27695. Cost at the time of this writing is $4.50.

areas. Fortunately, as Mary Jane McSwain, author of *Florida Gardening by the Sea* (University Press of Florida, 1997), points out, many of the delicate tropicals are relatively inexpensive and can be replaced with ease. She advises thorough watering when a freeze is forecast and again as soon as possible afterward. This counteracts the dehydrating effects of wind and cold weather on foliage.

Because soil in beach areas along these coasts is poor, gardeners in these areas, like their northern counterparts, should supplement the sandy soil with good topsoil and plenty of mulch. And remember that even drought-resistant plants need regular watering in the first year or two, until growth is well-established.

Tips for the Beach Gardener. Like novice gardeners everywhere, the novice gardener at the beach is likely to approach the task with more enthusiasm than expertise. Predicatably, the results are likely to be less than satisfactory.

Before you tackle the task of landscaping your beach house, find out what kinds of plants are most likely to thrive in your particular locale. Consult the references cited above as a rough guide. Then spend time taking note of the plants that appeal to you in your neighbors' gardens and discussing plant choices with local landscapers and nursery owners. You will probably be pleasantly surprised at the rich variety of trees, shrubs, grasses, and flowers that will make themselves happily at home in your beach garden.

Finally, a good source of information for the coastal gardener is the encyclopedic *Taylor's Guide to Seashore Gardening*, edited by Frances Tenenbaum (Houghton Mifflin, 1996). If you're ready to jump in with both feet, you might want to join a national organization for coastal plant-lovers organized by Pamela D. Jacobsen (P.O. Box 262, Feeding Hills, MA, 01030; E-mail at 103242.2424@compuserve.com).

INTERIOR MAINTENANCE

If you read the preceding sections carefully, you know that homes by the sea are particularly subject to exterior damage from the elements. In the case of rental properties, beach houses are also subject to interior damage from the people who help pay your mortgage — your guests.

Even though most guests can be counted on to treat your property with some degree of care and respect, accidents will happen, especially when large numbers of people congregate on vacation. Suitcases slam into walls, leaving unsightly smudges and taking chunks out of corners. Gooey wads of candy or gum form a permanent bond with upholstery fabric and wood surfaces. Drips and drops of nail polish appear on carpets, along with other strange stains of unknown origin.

MINIMIZING MESS AND MISHAPS

The proverbial ounce of prevention goes a long way, indeed, in a rental property at the beach. If, for example, you have had the foresight to have had your walls covered in what's called a "knock down" finish (see Chapter 2), minor insults will be much less visible than on smooth walls. If you have used semi-gloss or high-gloss latex paint in areas subject to water and grease spots, you will also have less in the way of maintenance chores; if you haven't, be sure to stipulate this kind of paint when it comes time to repaint.

When it comes time to repaint, give some thought to using the same color throughout the house, or at least using the same color in all rooms on the same level. This will simplify things when touch-ups are needed. And plan on doing touch-ups annually: in spite of your best efforts, scuffs and stains will appear and will need cosmetic work.

Corner protectors affixed to outside corners are a very good investment. Wooden strips which are painted or stained to match walls or trim (or clear plastic, if used over wall paper), corner protectors will blend into the decor and, by shielding vulnerable corners from inevitable nicks and bumps, will preserve the appearance of your paint and wallpaper.

Even the sturdiest furniture can use some protection from the occasional thoughtless guest. Dressers, night stands, and end tables, for example, should have a polyurethane finish. If you can't cover a surface with polyurethane, cover it with protective glass.

It's also wise to provide cleaning equipment for your guests so that they can take care of little spills and accidents as they occur. This is particularly important if you decide to allow pets in your home. Fill a sturdy plastic pail with a big scrub brush, a spray-bottle of carpet cleaner, a hefty sponge, and several old towels.

RENEWING, RESTORING, AND REVITALIZING

In less expensive beach cottages, guests will tolerate a bit of genteel shabbiness, as long as the place is clean and comfortable. But, if you have a beach house that rents for top dollar, the last thing you want to convey is a worn, down-at-the-heels image.

Furniture. In a beach house, you can expect upholstered furniture to take a beating from constant use. You can also expect stains from wet bathing suits, suntan lotion, and the occasional spilled drink or melted popsicle. It helps a bit, we think, if your welcome letter to guests includes a request that they refrain from serving popsicles and Kool-Aid in the house, since these stains are truly forever.

Keeping upholstered furniture looking good is much easier if you've had the foresight to buy sofas and chairs which can be easily slip-covered. Slip-covers are relatively inexpensive and can be dry cleaned with ease.

When you have slipcovers made for your furniture, we suggest that you order an extra set for each piece to avoid the hassle of repeating the process in a few years. We also suggest that you order an extra seat cover and support-pillow cover for each couch that you have slip-covered. The cost is nominal and you will have a replacement cover available in the event that one cover is damaged on both sides and therefore not usable.

And don't forget to order arm covers for all upholstered pieces at the time of purchase and for slip-cover sets made after that. Arm covers can be attached with special cork-screw-like fasteners available at notions counters to provide unobtrusive protection for the arms. Since the arms are apt to show soil and wear more quickly than other sections of upholstered furniture, this little bit of foresight can extend the life of your upholstery and slip-covers.

To keep the cost of slip-covers and re-upholstery down, consider ordering fabric from a discount supplier. These companies often advertise in the classified sections of house-and-home magazines. One firm we've been particularly happy with is **The Fabric Center** (call 508-343-4402 or fax 508-343-8139 for catalogue). They carry an enormous variety of good-quality fabrics at very reasonable prices and, to help you decide, they will send you big swatches for a nominal sum.

Fixtures and Accessories. If you have purchased a house in which the former owners used brass fixtures, such as towel rods and door knobs, you will have to put in some work to keep these fixtures looking presentable. An excellent product for restoring brass objects to their original shining appearance is **Extend-A-Finish Brass and Copper Cleaner**. This product, which is available in local stores or by calling the manufacturer at 800-331-0502, removes the protective lacquer usually applied to brass without harming the brass itself and restores a shine to the brass. Use is not quite as simple as the advertisement suggests — we've found that several applications may be needed on exterior brass fixtures that retain some of their original heavy lacquer. However, the product does the job very well and, when used with the same company's **Brass and Copper Protector** applied annually, will give very satisfactory results.

Keeping light fixtures sparkling clean can be a problem in a beach house, because the salt air leaves a film on glass. When it comes time to replace ceiling fixtures, either purchase those made of opaque glass such as Tiffany-style glass or buy fixtures which can be easily removed for cleaning.

Window treatments such as vertical blinds and mini-blinds take a particular beating at the beach. The life of cloth-covered vertical blinds, such as are used on sliding doors to decks, can be prolonged enormously by purchasing them from the factory covered with plastic edge-covers. These plastic sleeves will eventually discolor under the sun's harsh rays but you can then remove them and use the unprotected blinds for another couple of seasons before they will have to be replaced.

To clean mini-blinds, screw big hooks into an exterior crossbeam at the appropriate intervals needed to hang the blinds. Then, spray with an all-purpose household cleaner and rinse with a hose.

Carpets and Floors. If you have large expanses of carpet, your property manager will probably arrange to have the high-traffic areas of your carpets cleaned at least once during the season to remove unsightly drips and splotches that are bound to appear from normal wear and tear.

Prior to the opening of rental season, have all of the carpets professionally cleaned. If there are unattractive ripples and bulges, have the carpet re-stretched. For really stubborn stains even the professionals can't remove, we've had good luck with **Proven Solutions Carpet Spot Cleaner** (to order, call IMPROVEMENTS at 1-800-642-2112). We've also been happy with **Wizard All-Purpose Cleaner, Degreaser, and Stain Remover** (919-753-3054).

SPRING CLEANING

This term takes on a whole new meaning if you own a rental home at the beach. In addition to the deep-cleaning involved (e.g. carpets, blinds, drawers), spring cleaning should include preventive maintenance, as well. As we noted in Chapter 1, renters can be very picky, especially in high-end homes. To avoid costly maintenance visits during the season, it's important to be sure that all drains are clear and free of clogs, that dripping faucets are repaired, and that doors and locks open freely.

Unless you are willing to pay for spring cleaning services, be prepared to roll up your sleeves to tackle a long list of chores. In addition to vacuuming under and behind all furniture and cleaning the interior of every drawer and cabinet, your list should include the following:

> o   Wash all windows; remove and hose down all screens and mini-blinds.

> o   Wash or dry-clean curtains and drapes, as needed.

> o   Remove contents from all kitchen drawers and clean drawers.

o Clean the oven.

o Check all kitchen utensils and cooking equipment; replace as needed.

o Check caulking around all showers and bath tubs. Check grout where ceramic floor tiles abut tubs and showers to be sure that water can't leak and damage ceilings in rooms below.

o Check every appliance — even those you, yourself, never use — to be sure all are in good working order.

o Remove drain stoppers and check for hair balls which can lead to costly plumber's fees.

o Use a lubricant such as WD 40 on all locks and in the tracks of sliding doors.

o Replace all burnt-out light bulbs, inside and out.

o Clean out contents of dune decks and utility closets; replenish supplies as needed.

o Wash or dry clean all bed-spreads; wash mattress pads and pillow protectors.

o Wash or replace all shower-curtain liners.

Whether you do the spring cleaning yourself or have it done by your property management firm, one responsibility that you should take quite seriously is an annual inspection to be sure that your property is as free from hazards as you can make it. See Chapter 7 for suggestions.

WINTERIZING

In comparison to spring cleaning, winterizing your beach home in those coastal areas where winterizing is necessary is actually quite simple. Much of the work — that of draining the lines and traps and replacing water with anti-freeze, for example — will be done by the staff of your property management firm at a date you determine.

A complete winterizing program includes the following:

o Drain all water supply pipes and water heater; blow supply pipes clean with compressed air; put antifreeze in all drain traps.

o Turn off water at meter or drain pump.

o Turn off power at main breaker.

o Secure windows and doors.

o Place trash cans in protected areas.

For houses with pools and hot tubs, additional costs are incurred for winterizing.

If you have any light-weight deck furniture, don't forget to store it in a secure location such as a shed or in the outside shower stall. And, before you close the place for the winter, be sure to place rodent poison under sinks on every floor to hold the mouse and rat population down. Unchecked, these uninvited but inevitable little visitors will leave a nasty trail of droppings in cupboards and drawers and may well eat holes in your bedding, too.

Finally, your property-management firm may provide off-season security checks. Most firms will do this on a monthly basis to check for damage or evidence of break-ins. Should storms occur, the inspection should include a check for storm-related damage and leaks. Costs for this service vary by locale.

CHAPTER 7

LIMITING YOUR LIABILITY

PLANNING FOR SAFETY

No matter how much liability insurance you have, it's always a good idea to think through any potential hazards your property might hold for your paying guests. Not only do you not want to face a law-suit; you also don't want your guests to spoil their vacation by injuring themselves. By taking a few simple precautions, you can help insure a safe vacation for your guests.

   o **Avoid Dangerous Amenities**. The popular "reverse floor plan" that places general living areas at the top of the house means that guests must carry groceries and other necessities up two or even three flights of steps. Thus, many people who build luxury homes at the beach include elevators or dumbwaiters to spare themselves this chore. We're all for this — in fact, one of us has a dumbwaiter that we've come to consider a "must-have." In a rental home, however, while such amenities may increase the your house's appeal to potential renters, they can also be an invitation to a law-suit: what would your liability be, for example, if Johnny caught his arm in the elevator or stuffed his little sister in the dumbwaiter? If you do include such amenities for your own use, consider locking them securely with locks keyed to your owner's closets (**not** the main doors in the house) for when tenants are in residence.

Complicated and potentially dangerous exercise equipment falls into the same category. If you enjoy using such equipment but don't want to incur liability for injuries to your tenants, lock the equipment in a shed or owner's closet.

o **Provide Good Lighting**. Walkways, decks, and carports should be well-illuminated. It's thoughtful, too, to include night-lights in bathrooms and hallways.

o **Provide Safety Equipment**. If you provide bikes for your guests, you should also provide bike helmets, one per bike. If your home has a swimming pool, be sure to provide life-preservers and safety vests in a variety of sizes. Consider adding a fence around the pool, with a latch that is beyond the reach of small children.

Smoke detectors and fire extinguisher are both required by law but their location is dictated only by common sense. If you're smart, you'll place a fire extinguisher on every floor. Be sure to note the location of all fire extinguisher in your letter to your guests (see Chapter 5). As concerns smoke detectors, place them outside sleeping areas and on each additional floor. Do **not** place them near furnaces, water heaters, bathrooms, or kitchens, since fumes, smoke, and exhaust can trigger faulty alarms.

Although it is not required of you, it certainly is a humanitarian gesture to provide your guests with safety information about the beaches in your particular locale. Some beaches, such as those on the Outer Banks, for example, are particularly subject to rip tides and other dangerous conditions. This information is particularly important in beach resorts which do not have life guards on duty during the season.

o **Check for Hazards**. Make it a part of your spring ritual to check your house and grounds for potential hazards. If one of last year's tenants left a can of charcoal starter in the fish-cleaning area, remove it before a three-year-old guest finds it and — god forbid! — takes a swig.

Check the batteries in all smoke detectors. Check the temperature of your hot water to be sure that the water temperature is in the safe range so a guest doesn't scald himself while shaving or showering. Check your fire extinguishers, too. And don't forget to check for, and replace, any frayed cords on lamps or appliances. Finally, go over all decks and walkways with hammer in hand and pound in protruding nails which might have popped up over the winter.

LIMITED LIABILITY CORPORATION

Even though you will purchase general liability insurance for your beach house, the litigious conditions that exist in our society today demand that you look for ways to further minimize your liability as the owner of a vacation rental home. One way in which to do this is to establish a Limited Liability Company to hold your real estate.

There are three commonly-recognized business entities: C-Corporations, S-Corporations, and Partnerships. In most states, there is now a new business entity available, the Limited Liability Company ("LLC"). Like a corporation, an LLC offers limited liability. However, for tax purposes it is treated as a partnership, so you avoid double taxation. There is no limit on the number or type of members who can belong to an LLC: members can include corporations, partnerships, and trusts. An LLC allows for flexible allocation of income, deductions, and cash flow. This is an important point to discuss with your accountant or tax attorney, who can explain it in greater detail.

It is relatively simple to establish an LLC. At your request, you attorney merely files articles of organization with the State corporation Commission, indicating the name of the LLC, the registered agent, and the location of the principal office. You then deed your property (in this case, your beach house) to the LLC, after determining what percentage of the assets each member of the LLC will own (note that shares do not have to be apportioned on an equal basis).

ADVANTAGES OF AN LLC

Why should you consider establishing an LLC? In a nutshell, placing your beach house in an LLC limits your liability to the holdings of the LLC itself. If you should be sued by a tenant and found liable for a sum greater than that covered by your liability insurance, you can lose only those assets held by the LLC itself; that is, you cannot be forced to give up your primary residence, automobiles, or other assets not held in the LLC in order to satisfy the judgement against the LLC.

> **EXAMPLE** Sarah and Sam own a beach house that is in a rental program. They established an LLC and placed the house in the LLC. Thus, the LLC actually owns the house and Sarah and Sam are the shareholders of the LLC. The house is valued at $400,000 and liability insurance is for $500,000. A tenant falls down a stairwell, sustains a permanent injury to his back, and sues the owner of the house — that is, the LLC. The court finds the LLC liable because there was inadequate lighting in the stairwell and awards the tenant one million dollars in damages. The liability insurance covers $500,000 but the LLC must sell the beach house to pay the remainder of the judgement. However, if the beach house sells only for its assessed value of $400,000, Sarah and Sam are not personally liable for the remainder of the judgement.

There is another benefit, too, to establishing an LLC for your beach house: namely, an LLC provides the means by which parents can transfer property to their children while minimizing gift taxes. The tax code stipulates that you can give a gift of up to $10,000 per year without paying a gift tax. Thus, if you wanted to give your child a share of your $200,000 property without paying gift tax, you would deed over 5 percent of the property (worth $10,000). However, if this property were in an LLC you could actually give your child more than 5 percent of the assets without paying gift taxes.

Why is this the case? In the first place, you are transferring only an interest in the LLC, not the property itself. Secondly, tax courts have ruled that a 10-percent interest, for example, in an LLC is not actually worth 10 percent of the assets of the LLC, because it represents a minority interest in a property controlled by someone else. Thus, parents can retain control of the property as managers while equity value passes on to the children, but is also subject to less in the way of taxes.

In addition to these benefits, there are no limitations on the type of trust that can hold an interest in an LLC. Again, your CPA or tax attorney can explain the details to you.

AN LLC: IS IT RIGHT FOR YOU?

While you can place as many pieces of property into an LLC as you like, you must remember that all of the assets of an LLC are at risk in case of litigation. In the example above, if the LLC held additional property, it would have been sold to pay the remainder of the award.

LLCs are not without problems and drawbacks. For example, an LLC is considered terminated if 50 percent or more of the interest in its holdings changes hands in a twelve-month period — if, for example, your equal partner in an LLC dies, leaving his share to his estate. Then, too, when an LLC interest is transferred, the recipient receives only the rights to income and distributions: he or she has no say in the management of the LLC unless there is unanimous agreement among the other members that he/she can do so.

Laws governing LLCs vary from state to state. It's important, therefore, that you discuss all the pros and cons of establishing an LLC with your tax attorney. Only then can you be sure that an LLC is right for you.

PROTECTING YOUR UNOCCUPIED PROPERTY

Your paying guests aren't the only ones who have the potential to wreak havoc on your investment: burglars and vandals can also take a heavy toll if they select your home as a target. Therefore, as an absentee owner, you must give some thought to protecting your property when neither you nor your tenants are in residence.

It goes without saying that you should have adequate locks on all windows and exterior doors, as we discussed in Chapter 3. However, unless these locks are actually **locked**, they offer no protection. Obvious, no?

Yet, as Ruth Rejnis and Clair Walter point out,[*] surveys show that 42 percent of home burglaries don't involve forcible entry; instead, burglars just avail themselves of doors that have been left unlocked.

In addition to providing protection against wind-driven debris which hurricane winds can hurl through windows and doors, shutters can also provide security against intruders. Both rolling shutters and accordion shutters can be locked as a deterrent to burglars.

Rejnis and Walter also suggest that you look into a high-tech security system that will protect your home in your absence, particularly if you have an expensive home with many amenities and accoutrements. As they point out, some of these systems not only alert authorities when someone tries to force entry into your home; they will also send an alert if there is flooding, smoke or fire, or an electrical malfunction. Finally, they wisely advise that absentee owners check with the local police department about their safety guides for home owners. Our advice: be sure to check with your property management firm about their own security procedures to protect absentee owners.

---

[*] *Buying Your Vacation Home for Fun & Profit.* Dearborn Financial Publishing, Inc., 155 N. Wacker Drive, Chicago, IL 60606-1719 (800-621-9621).

APPENDICES

APPENDIX A

FURNISHING YOUR KITCHEN

In addition to china and glassware in sufficient quantity for your guests, your kitchen should contain the following basic items.

ELECTRICAL APPLIANCES

Drip coffemaker (two, in larger homes)
Toaster (four slice) or toaster oven with auto shut-off
Electric can opener
Blender
Hand mixer

COOKWARE

Covered sauce pan, 1-quart
Covered sauce pan, 2-quart
Covered sauce pan, 3-quart
Roasting pan
Dutch oven
Seafood steamer
Covered fry pan, 10"
Covered fry pan, 12"

Covered casserole, 2-quart
Baking dish, 3-quart
Cookie sheets
Muffin tins
Loaf pan
Pizza pan
Tea kettle

FOOD PREPARATION

Mixing bowls: 3 or 4, in graduated sizes
Measuring cup, spoons
Colander
Large cutting board
Cutlery set and holder (NOTE: either buy top quality or provide a knife
    sharpener)
Paper towel holder

KITCHEN TOOLS

Small turner
Large turner
Slotted spoon
Basting spoon
Cooking fork
Mixing spoons
Whisk
Ice cream scoop

Vegetable peeler
Can/bottle opener
Cork screw
3-way grater
Pizza cutter
Spatula set
Cooking tongs
Nut cracker

TABLE TOP

Stainless flatware
Dinner ware
Napkin holder
Salt and pepper
Bread basket
Trivets
Glass serving bowl, 10"
Vegetable bowl (2)
Meat platter

Salad bowl
Steak knives
Butter dish
Salad tongs
Place mats
Cream and sugar set

KITCHEN CLEAN-UP

Dish drainer and tray
Cutlery trays
Large trash can
Scouring pad
Dust pan

Pot holders
Broom
Mop
Fly swatter
Bucket, scrub brush

ACCESSORIES

Coffee carafe
Covered food storage containers

If your budget is flexible, you might want to upgrade your kitchen by including some of the following:

Coffee Bean grinder   Wine Carafe
Food Processor   Pasta machine
Espresso machine   Salad Spinner

APPENDIX B

MISCELLANEOUS HOUSEHOLD ITEMS

For the comfort, convenience, and safety of your guests, provide the following items.

    o Vacuum cleaner with extra bags

    o Iron and ironing board

    o Sponge mop

    o Laundry basket

    o Waste baskets in every room

    o Fire extinguisher

    o Scissors

    o Flashlight and batteries

    o First aid kit

    o Mini tool kit

    o Toilet plunger